FORT WORTH PUBLIC LIBRARY

3 1668 04255 0324

W9-BEP-490

CHILDREN 970.00497 IVERSON
   2006
Iverson, Peter
The Navajo

Central   08/09/2010

CENTRAL LIBRARY

The Navajo

Indians
of North
America

Heritage Edition

◄ Indians ►
of North
America

Heritage Edition

Indians
of North
America

The Navajo

Peter Iverson
with additional text written by
Jennifer Nez Denetdale

Foreword by
Ada E. Deer
University of Wisconsin-Madison

CHELSEA HOUSE
PUBLISHERS
An imprint of Infobase Publishing

COVER: Nineteenth-century Navajo blanket.

THE NAVAJO

Copyright © 2006 by Infobase Publishing

All rights reserved. No part of this book may be reproduced or utilized in
any form or by any means, electronic or mechanical, including photocopying,
recording, or by any information storage or retrieval systems, without permission
in writing from the publisher. For information contact:

Chelsea House
An imprint of Infobase Publishing
132 West 31st Street
New York, NY 10001

Library of Congress Cataloging-in-Publication Data

Iverson, Peter.
  The Navajo / Peter Iverson ; with additional text written by Jennifer Denetdale.
     p. cm. — (Indians of North America)
  Includes bibliographical references and index.
  ISBN 0-7910-8595-3 (hard cover)
  1. Navajo Indians—History—Juvenile literature. 2. Navajo Indians—Social life and
customs—Juvenile literature. I. Denetdale, Jennifer. II. Title. III. Indians of North
America (Chelsea House Publishers)
  E99.N3I883 2005
  979.1004'9726—dc22

                                                                2005007544

Chelsea House books are available at special discounts when purchased in
bulk quantities for businesses, associations, institutions, or sales promotions.
Please call our Special Sales Department in New York at (212) 967-8800 or
(800) 322-8755.

You can find Chelsea House on the World Wide Web at
http://www.chelseahouse.com

Series and cover design by Keith Trego

Printed in the United States of America

IBT EJB 9 8 7 6 5 4 3

All links and Web addresses were checked and verified to be correct at the time
of publication. Because of the dynamic nature of the Web, some addresses and
links may have changed since publication and may no longer be valid.

Contents

Foreword

Ada E. Deer

American Indians are an integral part of our nation's life and history. Yet most Americans think of their Indian neighbors as stereotypes; they are woefully uninformed about them as fellow humans. They know little about the history, culture, and contributions of Native people. In this new millennium, it is essential for every American to know, understand, and share in our common heritage. The Cherokee teacher, the Mohawk steelworker, and the Ojibwe writer all express their tribal heritage while living in mainstream America.

The revised INDIANS OF NORTH AMERICA series, which focuses on some of the continent's larger tribes, provides the reader with an accurate perspective that will better equip him/her to live and work in today's world. Each tribe has a unique history and culture, and knowledge of individual tribes is essential to understanding the Indian experience.

Prior to the arrival of Columbus in 1492, scholars estimate the Native population north of the Rio Grande ranged from seven to twenty-five million people who spoke more than three hundred different languages. It has been estimated that ninety percent of the Native population was wiped out by disease, war, relocation, and starvation. Today there are more than 567 tribes, which have a total population of more than two million. When Columbus arrived in the Bahamas, the Arawak Indians greeted him with gifts, friendship, and hospitality. He noted their ignorance of guns and swords and wrote they could easily be overtaken with fifty men and made to do whatever he wished. This unresolved clash in perspectives continues to this day.

A holistic view recognizing the connections of all people, the land, and animals pervades the life and thinking of Native people. These core values—respect for each other and all living things; honoring the elders; caring, sharing, and living in balance with nature; and using not abusing the land and its resources—have sustained Native people for thousands of years.

American Indians are recognized in the U.S. Constitution. They are the only group in this country who has a distinctive *political* relationship with the federal government. This relationship is based on the U.S. Constitution, treaties, court decisions, and attorney-general opinions. Through the treaty process, millions of acres of land were ceded *to* the U.S. government *by* the tribes. In return, the United States agreed to provide protection, health care, education, and other services. All 377 treaties were broken by the United States. Yet treaties are the supreme law of the land as stated in the U.S. Constitution and are still valid. Treaties made more than one hundred years ago uphold tribal rights to hunt, fish, and gather.

Since 1778, when the first treaty was signed with the Lenni-Lenape, tribal sovereignty has been recognized and a government-to-government relationship was established. This concept of tribal power and authority has continuously been misunderstood by the general public and undermined by the states. In a series of court decisions in the 1830s, Chief Justice John Marshall described tribes as "domestic dependent nations." This status is not easily understood by most people and is rejected by state governments who often ignore and/or challenge tribal sovereignty. Sadly, many individual Indians and tribal governments do not understand the powers and limitations of tribal sovereignty. An overarching fact is that Congress has plenary, or absolute, power over Indians and can exercise this sweeping power at any time. Thus, sovereignty is tenuous.

Since the July 8, 1970, message President Richard Nixon issued to Congress in which he emphasized "self-determination without termination," tribes have re-emerged and have utilized the opportunities presented by the passage of major legislation such as the American Indian Tribal College Act (1971), Indian Education Act (1972), Indian Education and Self-Determination Act (1975), American Indian Health Care Improvement Act (1976), Indian Child Welfare Act (1978), American Indian Religious Freedom Act (1978), Indian Gaming Regulatory Act (1988), and Native American Graves Preservation and Repatriation Act (1990). Each of these laws has enabled tribes to exercise many facets of their sovereignty and consequently has resulted in many clashes and controversies with the states and the general public. However, tribes now have more access to and can afford attorneys to protect their rights and assets.

Under provisions of these laws, many Indian tribes reclaimed power over their children's education with the establishment of tribal schools and thirty-one tribal colleges. Many Indian children have been rescued from the foster-care system. More tribal people are freely practicing their traditional religions. Tribes with gaming revenue have raised their standard of living with improved housing, schools, health clinics, and other benefits. Ancestors' bones have been reclaimed and properly buried. All of these laws affect and involve the federal, state, and local governments as well as individual citizens.

Tribes are no longer people of the past. They are major players in today's economic and political arenas; contributing millions of dollars to the states under the gaming compacts and supporting political candidates. Each of the tribes in INDIANS OF NORTH AMERICA demonstrates remarkable endurance, strength, and adaptability. They are buying land, teaching their language and culture, and creating and expanding their economic base, while developing their people and making decisions for future generations. Tribes will continue to exist, survive, and thrive.

Ada E. Deer
University of Wisconsin–Madison
June 2004

1

Into the Fourth World

Peoples all over the world tell stories about their beginnings. By repeating tales passed down by previous generations, a society's storytellers pass along a heritage as old as memory and as new as the youngest child within the community. The stories not only entertain, they instruct. They reinforce in the listeners a sense of the right way of doing things, the right way of behaving as a member of their society.

Good storytellers are like weavers. They gather together the various strands of a people's past and from them create patterns forming a complex but ultimately unified design. Different weavers fashion different styles of rugs. Yet, to the discerning eye, there can be no question about what kind of weaver made any particular rug. There may be imitations; there may be fakes. A real Navajo rug, however—the Navajo people are in fact renowned as master weavers—is one that cannot be mistaken. And a good Navajo rug, like the Navajo stories, like the people themselves, will last.

The Navajos are today the second-largest Indian *tribe* in North America. Their homeland occupies much of northeastern Arizona and portions of New Mexico and Utah. Yet they have not always been a large group, nor have they always lived in their current location. The Navajos' history is a story of both change and continuity. Their ancient tales help to explain who they have been and who they are now.

The Navajos' own story of their origin begins with a description of the emergence of all living things through a series of worlds. Some storytellers say the first world was black, the second blue, the third yellow, and call the fourth—the present world—glittering or bright. Others speak of fewer or more worlds. In all cases, the stories in some way emphasize the number four. Four is an important number for the Navajos, as it is for many other Indian groups. It reminds the Navajos of the four seasons, the four directions, the four sacred mountains of their territory, and other important aspects of tribal life.

The Navajos' emergence story provides its hearers with several lessons to guide them in life. The importance of harmony within a group of people is particularly stressed. In most versions, the main reason humans and other creatures have to move from one world to the next is that they cannot get along with one another. In one variation, men and women quarrel over a misunderstanding. The two groups then separate, but they do not prosper in each other's absence. Eventually the men and women reunite and thereafter have a better appreciation of the need to try to understand and tolerate the ways of the opposite sex.

In all four worlds, humans coexist with insects and animals. These include squirrels, turkeys, lizards, and deer creatures familiar to the Navajos of today. These animals' presence during the emergence journey implies that people are not superior to, or meant to live independent of, other forms of life.

The animals in the Navajos' *origin story* have particular characteristics. The most prominent example is Coyote. Coyote

Until the mid-twentieth century, Navajos relied on oral history to pass down their sacred stories from generation to generation. Shown here are two Navajo men conversing in 1914.

is a trickster and a joker whose antics inevitably result in problems for others. Coyote plays a similar role in the Navajos' many stories about him in this world.

When all beings finally emerge into the present world, they find that it is covered entirely with water. They manage, however, to come to terms with a monster who controls the waters, so that eventually the waters withdraw and the world known to the Navajos today begins to form. The four sacred mountains that mark the traditional boundaries of Navajo country take shape: San Francisco Peak (also known as Abalone Shell Mountain) in the west, Blanca Peak (Dawn or White Shell Mountain) in the east, Mount Taylor (Blue Bead or Turquoise Mountain) in the south, and Mount Hesperus (Obsidian Mountain) in the north.

As the story is commonly told, it is at this time that the sun, moon, and stars first appear in the sky, day and night come to be, and the year divides into seasons. This is also the period during which the First Man and the First Woman arrive in the vicinity of what is now called Huerfano Mountain in New Mexico. A baby is then born of the mingling of darkness and dawn at Gobernador Knob, a geologic formation in northeastern New Mexico. First Man and First Woman find the baby after they hear her cry one morning at dawn. Together, they rear the infant with the aid of instructions from sacred spirits known as the Holy People. The child grows up to be Changing Woman, who is said to have arrived in the Navajo world at this time because only then was it ready for her. With the four sacred mountains and all plants and animals in their proper places, the world has achieved a kind of beauty and harmony, which, the storytellers note, is the opposite of the chaos found in the previous worlds.

When Changing Woman reaches puberty, the Holy People conduct a ceremony for her so that she may walk in beauty as an adult. This ritual, called the *kinaalda*, is still performed for young Navajo women. This is another example of how the origin story explains elements of contemporary Navajo life.

Later in the story, Changing Woman falls asleep by a waterfall, where she is visited by the Sun. She then becomes pregnant and gives birth to twin sons. She names one Child Born of Water and the other Monster Slayer. The two boys grow hardy by getting up before sunrise and running and by rolling in the snow. They also learn to hunt. During their childhood, Changing Woman creates the corn plant. Later, she mixes cornmeal with scrapings of her own skin to create the first Navajo people.

While hunting one day, Changing Woman's two sons see a small hole in the ground. A voice coming from the hole urges them to go inside it. The hole magically grows wider, and they descend into it, using a ladder they find awaiting them. Inside, they meet another legendary figure of the Navajo people, Spider Woman. (Later, she will teach the Navajos how to weave.)

The boys ask Spider Woman who their father is, because their mother has always refused to tell them. Spider Woman says only that she knows his identity and will assist them in finding him. She also explains to them that their father could help them destroy the monsters who have been plaguing all people on earth. But before they can reach their father, the boys will have to undergo a long, difficult, and dangerous journey.

Because Child Born of Water and Monster Slayer have grown strong through proper living, they are well prepared for their ordeal. Yet they cannot reach the Sun unaided. In order to survive the journey, they learn from Spider Woman about the obstacles that await them. She teaches the twins special prayers and explains to them carefully what they will encounter and how to prevent disaster. To see their father, Monster Slayer and Child Born of Water will have to avoid or overcome four hazards on their way to the Sun's residence, then maneuver past four more hazards guarding his domain.

Armed with this knowledge, the boys are able to get by the reeds that cut the unwary traveler and cause him to bleed to death. They successfully cross the sands that can shift and smother a wanderer. They barely elude being crushed by a canyon that threatens to close in on all who pass through it. Finally, by taking an alternate route to the south, they bypass four rock columns that have the power to turn them into withered old men.

Before the twins reach the Sun's home, they enlist the assistance of a worm and a water bug to transport them across a bog and an ocean. Monster Slayer and Child Born of Water then come to the obstacles guarding the Sun's residence—the great snake, the enormous black bear, the big thunder, and the big wind. By chanting the prayers Spider Woman taught them, the twins safely gain entrance.

Suddenly faced by the twins, the Sun refuses to accept that

they are his children. He says he cannot be their father, in part because he does not want his wife to know that he might have impregnated another woman. The Sun tells the boys he will believe they are his sons only if they go through still another series of dangerous physical ordeals.

After the twins manage to survive these, the Sun, true to his word, admits that he is their father. To reward them for passing his tests, the Sun offers the boys wonderful things—including corn, horses, and jewels—from the four rooms of his house. But Child Born of Water and Monster Slayer say they want only his help in killing the monsters. The Sun then gives them each a particular type of lightning to use to destroy their enemies and flint armor to wear for protection.

The Navajos tell many stories of the great adventures the twins had as they sought to slaughter the monsters. For example, in one tale, they kill an incredible giant. When the giant falls, he bleeds profusely. The black lava flow near present-day Grants, New Mexico, is said to be the giant's dried blood. The twins also shoot and kill a monstrous bird that had resided on top of another Navajo country landmark—an isolated mountain in northwestern New Mexico known as Shiprock. Tellers of these stories explain that the world became safe for the Navajo people to inhabit because of the brothers' heroism. But they also remind their listeners that the twins triumphed only because they were given help from many others, including Spider Woman, the Sun, and such seemingly insignificant creatures as the worm and the water bug.

The Navajos' stories about their origins emphasize that the people's association with their current surroundings dates back to the very beginnings of humankind. But the passages from one world to the next and the many journeys, trials, and adventures described in the various tales may also be seen as the story of an extended migration. Interpreted in this way, the tales are like a mythic mirror of the Navajos' own early history, based on what *archaeologists* and *linguists* have concluded about how the

Shiprock, or Tsé Bit' A'í (rock with wings), is located in northwestern New Mexico and plays an important role in Navajo legend. According to one story, Child Born of Water and his twin brother, Monster Slayer, killed a monstrous bird that lived on top of the nearly 1,800-foot monolith in order to make the world safe for the Navajos. Shown here are two Navajo horsemen near the base of Shiprock in an early-twentieth-century photo.

tribe came to inhabit what is now the southwestern United States.

Archaeologists are scientists who study the past as revealed by the objects left behind by past societies. Many archaeologists believe that North and South America were populated by the descendants of people who thousands of years ago migrated from Asia across the Bering Strait into what is now Alaska. Over time, humans gradually wandered southward, and eventually they inhabited lands throughout the two continents.

Archaeologists also believe that the Navajo people lived for a very long time in far northern North America. In their judgment, two thousand years ago the Navajos still resided in what is now northwestern Canada or Alaska.

Approximately five hundred years ago, the Navajos had probably become residents of the Southwest. The exact route the Navajos took to their new home and the precise date of their arrival there remain subject to debate. However, linguists (scholars of human languages) have a theory about the tribe's migration. They classify the Navajo language as part of a group of related languages known as the Athapaskan family. (Athapaska is a lake in northwestern Canada.) Other *Athapaskan languages* include those spoken by Indian groups who today live in the subarctic, as well as those spoken by some other peoples, such as the Hupas, who inhabit various locations scattered between there and the Southwest. Of the many Indian tribes now living in the Southwest, only the Apaches are related linguistically to the Navajos. Therefore, linguists argue that the Apaches and the Navajos were once a single group and probably did not separate until after they had come to their present location. In fact, the Navajos' name is a shortened form of the original Spanish name for them, Apaches de Nabajó (Apaches of the Nabajó). The word *Nabajó* may originally have been a place name or may have been an Indian term meaning "planted fields."

People who move bring with them their *culture*—that is, their society's way of life, with its own special beliefs, rituals, behavior patterns, and means of survival. These traditions influence the choices they make about how they lead their new lives. This abstract cargo, often referred to as "cultural baggage," is as important to immigrants' survival as the physical possessions they pack. But once they arrive at their destination, they face decisions, often difficult ones, about which elements of this baggage they must discard and which they may profitably keep. The Navajos retained one of the most central elements of their cultural baggage—their language—when they came to their new home. They might conceivably have adopted another language, just as immigrants to the United States today often learn English. But when the Navajos arrived in the Southwest, no one language dominated the region, for there were relatively few people and no single controlling group in the area. It is not surprising that, given no compelling reason to change, they kept their language.

In other matters, the Navajos faced more complicated choices. Today, technology sometimes allows people to maintain a certain way of life even in a normally hostile environment. For example, people from Ohio who move to the desert land of southern Arizona can maintain a grassy lawn through irrigation. But the Navajos of five hundred years ago did not have the luxury of such technology. When they moved to an environment radically different from that of northern North America, they had to confront without buffers the dilemma of change. Although they had probably been able to maintain most elements of their old culture during their long migration south, they had to decide how best to adapt to the world they encountered once they arrived in their new home.

In the northern regions, the Navajos had obtained food by hunting wild game, fishing, and gathering wild plants. They had made bows and arrows and harpoons to kill their prey. The Navajos also built wooden enclosures, into which they drove large game, such as elk and caribou, so that the trapped animals could be slaughtered more easily. They made clothing and cone-shaped houses from the skins of the animals they hunted. As they moved from place to place in search of game and wild vegetation, they wore snowshoes and used tame dogs to haul their goods on sleds. Although they did not make pottery, they did make baskets from tree bark. Usually they lived in small, loosely organized groups that *anthropologists* call bands. Their religious leaders were charged with the responsibility of mediating with the forces of nature and curing the sick.

Some aspects of this way of life transferred satisfactorily to the high desert country of the Southwest. But fishing and hunting many species of animals became less important because some fish and game were not plentiful in the Navajos' new home. New forms of transportation had to be developed that were appropriate to the rugged terrain. New clothing suitable for a hotter, drier climate had to be fashioned from available materials. Eventually, new types of dwellings were also devised.

Of course, these transformations did not occur overnight or in a season or even over a generation. But as the Navajos' migration over thousands of miles had already demonstrated, they were willing to accept change if necessary. Perhaps the most crucial adaptations the Navajos were forced to make were in their system of beliefs. Like most peoples all over the world, they had considered particular geographical features in their northern home to be sacred. Certain mountains, valleys, and lakes, therefore, were firmly linked to their concept of the meaning of their lives. After they arrived in the Southwest, the Navajos had to come to terms with nothing less than a new Earth and a new sky. This meant that they also had to redefine their ideas about who they were.

The Navajos responded by literally creating the world anew. With their origin story, they invested sacred significance in the majestic mountains they found in the Southwest. They identified specific places as the locations of events—such as the birth of Changing Woman—that had great importance to them as a people. Through this gradual process, the Navajos in effect said to their children: This is where we belong and where we will remain.

The Navajos did not have to evaluate and adjust their old culture in complete isolation, however, because when they came to the Southwest they did not come to an unpopulated land. Some Indian peoples had already lived there for centuries. Given the Navajos' adaptability, they were willing to learn from others, selectively adopting features of other societies that they found attractive or useful. Through this process, they could take some-thing into their culture and, in the course of many years, make it Navajo. This cultural flexibility allowed them to prosper.

Initially, the Navajos probably were most influenced by the people living closest to them. These people, today known as the

Pueblos, lived in many independent villages along the Rio Grande in what is now northern New Mexico, as well as in several isolated locations on the Colorado Plateau. Having migrated into the region from a northeastern direction, the Navajos first came into contact with the Pueblo people in what is now northwestern New Mexico. The Navajos, who call themselves *Diné* (the People), still call this region *Dinétah* (the Land of the People).

Some of the Pueblos had arrived in the Southwest as early as nine hundred years before the Navajos. By the time of the Navajo migration, these Pueblos had already come to terms with the land and had even learned to thrive in this arid and craggy environment. The Pueblos were good farmers. Although the Navajos probably had some contact with agricultural communities while traveling to the Southwest, they must have been impressed with the Pueblos' ability to grow corn, melons, and other crops. Over the years, the Pueblos had become so familiar with the terrain, climate, and seasonal changes that they were adept at farming using little water.

The Pueblo farmers' reliable source of food must have been esteemed tremendously by the Navajos, who in the north had had to travel constantly in search of animals to hunt and wild plants to gather. A successful farming community offers its inhabitants security and stability. Most important, it provides freedom from the fear of starvation, perhaps the greatest of all fears. It also allows a people to stay in one place for a long period of time.

In addition to the Pueblos, the Navajo people also came into contact with the Hopis, living in what is now northern Arizona. But as fortune and fate would have it, the Hopis and other Pueblo Indian communities were soon not the only source for additions to the Navajos' culture. Not long after the Navajos arrived in their new home, people from another society on the other side of the world began to have an influence in the Southwest. In far-off Spain, business interests, curiosity

The Spanish introduced sheep to the Navajos in the early 1700s and by the end of the century, sheep had become an integral part of Navajo life. Today, sheep remain an important part of the Navajo economy—their wool is used for clothing and blankets, and their meat is used for sustenance. Shown here is a Navajo sheepherder near Navajo National Monument, Arizona.

about the distant country of Cathay (China), and improvements in sailing vessels all combined to encourage an era of exploration. By the end of the 1400s, Spain's queen, Isabella I, gave the Italian explorer Christopher Columbus the financial backing he needed to search for a new trade route to China. But Columbus' ships accidentally sailed instead to a world new to him and all other Europeans. The lives of all the Native peoples of North and South America would be permanently altered.

After Columbus' voyage, the Spanish became the first great European colonizers by promptly dispatching explorers, traders, settlers, and missionaries to what is now Mexico, South

America, and the western United States. Of course, not all Spanish colonists had exactly the same objectives, and their actions and priorities were not the same in all areas. Nonetheless, they all brought their own cultural baggage to their new home, which they called New Spain. This included their own language, religion (Christianity), dress, housing, and system of government. Even when the colonists confronted Indian societies, many Spaniards tended to think that they were moving into a world where no culture existed. To them, people who did not worship God through the Catholic Church, speak Spanish, wear European-style clothing, observe the practice of church-sanctioned marriage, and live in European-style housing could not be considered civilized.

Spanish colonists had the most immediate impact on Indian groups that had well-established settlements, such as the Pueblos. Populous Pueblo villages proved to be prime sites for the establishment of *missions* by Spanish priests who came to the Southwest to convert the Indians to Christianity. But those Indian peoples, including the Navajos, who ranged over a wide territory, felt the Spanish presence only fitfully. For instance, if a Spanish missionary tried to compel a Navajo to attend Mass, the Navajo could simply travel to a remote area of the tribe's lands to avoid the service.

Although few Navajos went to Mass or learned to speak Spanish fluently, the tribe did choose to incorporate some elements of Spanish culture into its own. Along with their religious teachings, the missionaries brought European fruits and vegetables—such as peaches, potatoes, and wheat—and the knowledge of how to grow them. Spaniards also introduced to the region cattle, sheep, and horses, all of which would become very important to the Navajos. Indeed, the raising of sheep became central to the Navajo way of life. Today, it is difficult to imagine the Navajos living without large herds of sheep.

Ironically, the Spanish, who eventually destroyed the culture of many Indian groups in their conquest of North and

South America, provided the Navajos with some of the key elements of their cultural identity. These very additions to the tribe's culture enabled it to become a major force in the Southwest. In 1492, when Columbus first crossed the Atlantic Ocean, few if any of the people of the region could have predicted that the immigrant Navajos would emerge as such an important Indian group. But the culture of New Spain, like the offspring of darkness and dawn, helped make the Navajo people's emergence into this new world possible.

2

The Evolution of Navajo Culture

The Navajos are often called a tribe—a term that is usually used to describe a group of individuals who are politically and economically united. The Navajos, however, did not become a cohesive people until the mid-nineteenth century, more than two centuries after their first contact with the Spanish. During this two-hundred-year period, most of the distinguishing features of their culture—those now considered distinctly Navajo—evolved. Some attributes of Navajo culture are easily perceived, such as the objects and animals the Navajos found to be of enduring value to them as a people. Other attributes are abstract and invisible but no less important. These include the beliefs, ceremonies, and social relationships that bound all Navajos to their community and imposed order, meaning, and purpose on their existence.

At birth, Navajo children became valued members of both their family and the larger community. Navajo parents placed their babies in cradleboards, beds made of a wooden platform and leather straps that were tied around the infants to keep them securely contained. Strapped in cradleboards, babies could be carried easily by their parents as they performed their daily activities. From this niche, infants watched the members of their family and learned how they lived and worked together. In time, young children came to realize that they belonged to this group and were expected eventually to contribute to its well-being. In Navajo society, the individual did matter, but primarily as a part of a larger social unit.

Navajo children were raised by the members of an extended family. Grandparents, aunts, uncles, and older siblings all played roles in a child's upbringing. Boys learned skills such as hunting, tracking, and ceremonial activities, and girls became adept at cooking, weaving, and similar domestic duties. Young Navajos were expected to learn from and emulate their elders. Both girls and boys, therefore, did not have to look far for role models for the responsibilities and privileges they would assume or enjoy later in life. Although children came to understand that living meant coping with change, they could also depend on a certain amount of continuity in their world.

Early in life, Navajo children learned that people rose before the sun. Their first glimpse of the new day was usually from their house, now called a *hogan*. In the subarctic, the early Navajos had used a pole or forked stick to prop up their hide-covered dwellings. In the Southwest, similarly, they used a pole or stick to help bolster a new kind of dwelling that they built primarily from earth. Over the generations, hogan builders came to use logs and strips of bark to create a cone- or dome-shaped skeleton that they covered with a thick coat of mud. A hole was left in the dwelling's wall to function as a doorway. These entrances always faced east, so that families received the Holy People's blessings each morning.

Each hogan had only a single room, which measured somewhere between twenty and thirty feet in diameter. The Navajos

Navajos resided in hogans, which were dome-shaped dwellings made of logs and mud. These single-room homes had one opening, which faced east toward the rising sun so that the Navajos could receive the blessing of the Holy People each morning.

spent much of their time outdoors, but the unpredictable and sometimes harsh climate of the Southwest often forced them to stay within their hogans for extended periods of time. Because family members of all ages shared this small space, they all had to be careful to pick up after themselves, keep their own possessions (such as clothes and hunting equipment) in order, and observe and respect the needs of others. Families developed a strategy for where things belonged both within their hogan and in the area immediately around it. During the summer and early autumn, clothing, blankets, and items for cooking were kept outside and brought inside only as needed.

Although the Navajos, unlike the Pueblos, did not live in villages, people generally found it convenient to build their homes near their relatives. With this arrangement, the members of an

extended family could work together to raise crops and livestock.

A young woman usually wed soon after reaching puberty.
A marriage was commonly arranged by a woman's family and
that of her prospective husband, who was often somewhat
older than the bride-to-be. Because marriage was usually a life-
long proposition, families took the matter very seriously and
discussed it among themselves. Although the practice was not
common, an older man who had accumulated some wealth
might have more than one wife. Because the family relationship
played a large role in most marriages, a widow might also
marry her deceased husband's brother.

Young married couples usually went to live in the vicinity
of the wife's mother. This woman or another female elder set
the rules of behavior for the individuals living in a cluster of
hogans. She served as the center of a world in miniature, one
that included a herd of sheep, the land used by the people of the
group, their homes, and perhaps fields of corn and other vegetables or fruits, which were cared for by both men and women.

In this close-knit group, everyone—children and adults—
had to mind how they acted because if a person misbehaved, it
reflected badly on both them and their kin. A Navajo saying
that is probably hundreds of years old describes someone who
behaves inappropriately as acting as though he does not have
any relatives.

All Navajos also belonged to a *clan*, a larger group of relatives who believed that they had descended from a common
ancestor. Husbands and wives always belonged to different
clans because fellow clan members were considered to be too
closely related to produce healthy children.

Navajo society is today divided into about sixty clans, the
members of which are scattered throughout the millions of
acres the Navajos now call home. These clans include
Todichi'iinii (Bitter Water), *Ashiihi* (Salt People), *To'aheedliinii*
(Water Flowing Together), *Kinyaa'aanii* (Towering House

People), and *Tl'izilani* (Many Goats). The name Tl'izilani indicates that some new clans came into existence over time, because the Navajos had goats only after the arrival of the Spanish in the 1500s.

Navajo children were born into their mother's clan—a system of descent known as *matrilineal*—but they also felt a special bond to the members of their father's clan. The tie between a mother and her children, however, was the deepest and most significant of any bond between relatives in Navajo society.

Given the importance of the mother-child tie and the likelihood that a married couple would live near the woman's mother, a Navajo husband and his mother-in-law often had a tense relationship. The Navajos found a fairly effective means to deal with this problem: A man usually tried never to speak to or even look at his wife's mother. Although this behavior did not entirely eliminate all confrontations, it did tend to make them less common and less serious.

By the late 1700s, the Navajo way of life revolved around the tribe's sheep herds. Their sheep were grazed in common but were owned by individual Navajos, who sometimes earmarked their animals and often knew them simply by sight. Most men and women owned at least a few, so virtually everyone had a direct interest in the herds' well-being. Parents gave their children lambs to look after and explained that these young sheep represented the beginning of the flock they would own as adults. By caring for these animals, children became working, integral members of the larger community very early in life.

Sheep served many purposes. Once a year, in the spring, men and women used knives to shear the sheep of their wool. The wool was traditionally used by Navajo women to weave blankets. After the arrival of European traders, Navajo women commonly wore dresses of woven cloth. By the late 1800s, Navajo blankets and rugs had become vital items of trade and sale in their economy. But long before that time, Navajo weavers made blankets for their family members. As the

Navajos became familiar with the natural resources of the Southwest, they discovered plants, shrubs, trees, and cacti that yielded dyes that could be used to color spun wool. They soon learned how to weave the dyed wool to create bold designs.

Sheep were also a source of meat—both lamb (from a young animal) and mutton (from an adult sheep). Mutton was frequently the tougher and less tasty of the two. Mutton was often cooked with vegetables such as potatoes, and other ingredients to make a stew. Navajos might eat this yummy stew with fried bread made with flour from their wheat harvest.

Navajos fed their sheep not only to their immediate family but also on occasion to other tribe members. The tribe placed a great value on generosity and on paying back the generous acts of others. It was therefore crucial for a person to be able to feed visiting clan members. Having enough extra meat to serve guests was also evidence of an individual's ability to tend his or her flock.

Meat from sheep was eaten at religious functions as well. Either alive or butchered, these animals often served as payment to a ceremonial singer for his service at a ritual. The Navajos believed that good things did not come free and that such payments had to be made if a ceremony were to be successfully performed.

The Navajos' spiritual beliefs were not a religion in the conventional sense. That term is in many ways too narrow to describe what the Navajos believed and practiced. Some understanding of the tribe's beliefs may be gained through consideration of a single Navajo word—*hózhó*. Hózhó is the combination of many ideas, including beauty, happiness, harmony, and goodness. It summarizes the basic goal and ultimate value of the Navajo world.

As recorded in the tribe's own stories of emergence, the Navajos knew that the world was fragile and that hózhó was difficult to achieve and maintain. The world included a great many good things, but it also contained much evil. Some potentially evil things—such as snakes, bears, and lightning—had to be contained or controlled, because they were harmful if not dealt with properly.

The Navajos believed that all people, knowingly or otherwise, could fall under the contaminating influence of these elements. Many rituals of Navajo ceremonies were meant to help people overcome such influences and restore hózhó. These rituals were performed to heal particular patients and were presided over by singers, whom non-Indians might view as both doctors and priests. The rites performed by singers are known as *chantways*.

Navajo ceremonies were extremely complex and therefore very difficult for novices to learn and memorize flawlessly. Some of the most elaborate ones took a full nine days to perform. A young man wishing to become a singer apprenticed himself to an experienced man who knew a particular ceremony or a few ceremonies. (Because of their great complexity, no one knew all the chantways.) The rituals had to be learned properly and then performed exactly right to achieve the desired effect. The Navajos believed that the chantways attracted the attention of the Holy People. If these supernatural beings judged that a chantway was being performed correctly, they would reciprocate by curing the patient.

Because a person's life could be disrupted in numerous ways, many ceremonies came to exist for restoring hózhó. Navajos suffering from poor health, uneasiness, or bad luck would consult with a man or woman who had the power to diagnose their problem and prescribe an appropriate ritual to cure them. For example, a man could become unbalanced if he wandered into the pueblo-like ruins of the villages of the Anasazis, a people who had vanished from the Southwest before the Navajos had migrated from the north. One ceremony that was commonly employed for this type of problem was the *nidah'*, known to non-Indians as the squaw dance. According to the Navajos' ancient stories, this ceremony originated when

Monster Slayer, one of Changing Woman's two sons, fell ill. The Holy People and the Navajos themselves created the nidah' to heal him.

The nidah' was held over six days and involved a lead singer and his helpers, the patient, the patient's family members who sponsored the ritual, and other relatives and friends. Although the nidah' was designed primarily to cure an ill person, it also brought people together because many people had to work cooperatively to make it possible. They had to pay ceremonial leaders, build temporary shelters for visitors, feed those in attendance, and gather gifts to offer the participants. Thus the nidah', like religious ceremonies the world over, was also a social function.

Some Navajo rituals were performed not to restore hózhó but to promote it. These rituals presented people with good wishes and protected them from evil. One example of such a ritual was the *Blessingway rite*, a core observance of the Navajos' traditional beliefs. Variations of the Blessingway rite were performed for many different purposes, such as protecting sheep herds, blessing a new marriage, helping an expectant mother in childbirth, giving strength to an apprentice singer, or shielding a warrior from his enemies.

The Blessingway rite generally began at sundown and was performed without interruption over the course of two nights and one day. During the first night, participants recited prayers and songs while the beneficiary of the ceremony held a sacred bundle, called the mountain soil bundle, to his or her chest. This bundle, made of buckskin, contained smaller packets, each holding small scoops of earth from the tops of the four sacred mountains. More songs and prayers were said the following day. The Blessingway rite concluded with the participants singing throughout the final night.

One version of the Blessingway rite was the kinaalda, the four-day ceremony performed for Navajo girls when they reached puberty and before they married. It not only blessed a young Navajo woman but also gave her the chance to learn from older women about their expectations for her as an adult. Traditionally, these expectations included being a good mother and wife, a skilled weaver, and a strong, patient, responsible person. During each day of the kinaalda, a girl would leave the hogan where the ceremony took place at dawn and run for a considerable distance, thus literally following in the footsteps of untold numbers of women before her. During the ceremony, which was arranged by each girl's mother, the young woman received much advice from older women about married life. The kinaalda was a happy occasion, and through it a young Navajo woman became an integral and important member of her people in both her own eyes and those of her family and community.

In some curative Navajo ceremonies, a *drypainting* (also called a sand-painting) was made by a helper under the supervision of the singer. These images were not actually formed with paint, but with dry pigments made from pulverized white, yellow, and red sandstone and crushed charcoal. The powders were shaped by the helper into patterns on the floor of the patient's hogan. Drypaintings ranged in size from less than one to more than twenty feet in diameter, took many hours to create, and were actively used in the final portion of the ceremony. The singer put his palms, moistened with herbal medicine, on top of the drypainting. After the painting's images were transferred to his hands, he placed his palms on the patient's body. This act linked the patient with the drypainting's sacred figures and thus assisted the healing process. At the end of the ceremony, the singer had what remained of the drypainting destroyed. After a drypainting was used in a ritual, the Navajos believed its reason for existence had come to an end.

In the years following the Navajos' migration to the Southwest, they lived in small communities spread over a wide territory. These communities were connected only loosely for political and military purposes. Sometimes a local leader would

Drypaintings, which range in size from less than one foot to more than twenty feet in diameter, are an important part of Navajo curing ceremonies and are used to request the deities' help in healing. The figures in the painting represent important stories in Navajo mythology.

come to speak for several communities or lead a large group of people into battle against other Indian groups (especially the Utes to the north) or, later, against the Spanish. But although the various Navajo communities shared a single culture, they did not compose one political state or military unit. There was no one chief for all the people.

By the early seventeenth century, the Navajos had acquired

horses, and their mobility increased. This permitted them to graze their sheep over a wider range and drive them into the shade of the mountains during the summer months. It also enabled them to not only to defend themselves from slave raiders but also to respond in kind to other Indian people or the Spanish colonists who raided them for slaves, food, horses, and other goods.

Soon the Navajos pushed westward into lands claimed by the Spanish in what is now New Mexico and Arizona. The tribe generally avoided contact with the colonists, who were still largely concentrated in communities near Pueblo settlements along the Rio Grande. However, the Navajos did have some relations with Spanish people. Navajo children were sometimes baptized in the Catholic Church, for example, and Navajo people taken captive in military raids were sometimes sold into slavery. Despite this contact with Christianity and European culture, the Navajo people maintained many of their traditional customs.

In 1680, many Pueblo Indians rebelled against the religious, political, and economic control of the colonizing Spaniards. Led by a man named Popay from San Juan Pueblo in present-day northern New Mexico, the Pueblos attacked the Spanish settlements in their territory and killed many of the inhabitants. The Pueblos then drove the survivors south. However, the Spanish soon returned to the region seeking revenge. Some Pueblos then fled from their homes and relocated on Navajo lands. Despite language differences, communication increased between the Pueblos and the Navajos, as did the influences each group had on the other's way of life.

Today it is often difficult to tell who learned what from whom. It is known, however, that some Navajo men married women from such communities as Jemez Pueblo, and their descendants incorporated elements of Pueblo culture into the daily lives of the Navajos. Because many Pueblo people were skilled farmers, the Navajos may have learned ways to improve their agricultural methods from this association, even though they themselves had been farming for generations prior to the Pueblo Revolt.

In the early eighteenth century, corn became a central element of Navajo culture, both as a food and as a symbol, after it was introduced by the Pueblos. Corn pollen came to be used in Navajo ceremonies, often to represent fertility or prosperity. The growth of the cornstalk was likened to the growth of the Navajo people themselves. In the tribe's stories, it associated the plant with the Holy People. The planting of corn thus was linked with the Navajos' origin.

The tribe's adoption of other Indian people, new crops, and European livestock during the 1600s and 1700s was key to the development of modern Navajo culture. The Navajos expanded and thrived because they took in elements of other cultures. Over the course of time, they even came to associate many of these relatively recent cultural acquisitions with their earliest days. They made them part of their legendary past. They made them Navajo.

During these same years, the descendants of the original Spanish colonists grew in number and became increasingly independent of their mother country. In the early 1800s, these people revolted against Spanish control and founded the modern nation of Mexico. At that time, Mexico extended into much of western North America, including what are now the states of Texas, New Mexico, Arizona, Colorado, Utah, Nevada, and California. But the vast majority of the Mexican population in the early nineteenth century resided south of this area. The non-Indian population of the Southwest remained sparse.

In the turmoil following its revolt against Spain, the new nation of Mexico was poorly equipped to defend the northernmost stretches of its borders. In early 1836, settlers in Texas revolted in turn against the Mexican government and established the Republic of Texas. At the request of the republic's citizens, the United States annexed Texas in 1845. However,

Mexico refused to acknowledge the legality of the annexation. In the conflict that ensued—the Mexican War of 1846–48—the United States won a crushing victory. It promptly seized the entire Southwest, allowing American settlers to journey westward into this region.

By the mid-nineteenth century, Americans had begun to arrive in Navajo country. Fortunately, the Navajos had established over hundreds of years a firm foundation for their own culture. But the Americans were soon to present an unparalleled challenge to the Navajo cultural world.

3

The
Long
Walk

On February 2, 1848, the Mexican War came to an end when Mexico and the United States signed the Treaty of Guadalupe Hidalgo. Under its terms, the Mexican government ceded to the United States more than 1.2 million square miles of territory, including much of present-day New Mexico, Arizona, Colorado, Utah, Nevada, and California, in exchange for $15 million and other considerations. The two sides gave no thought, however, to the Indian people who had lived in the Southwest long before either nation had even existed.

The Treaty of Guadalupe Hidalgo brought rapid change to the Navajo world. American settlers swiftly began to travel westward to the new lands the United States had acquired. Just as quickly, the U.S. government moved to exert control over the Southwest. On August 31, 1849, U.S. representatives James Calhoun and Colonel John Washington, accompanied by some U.S. soldiers, held a

Navajo chief Narbona (Tachíí'níí), shown here in an 1849 sketch by Richard Kern, helped lead the Navajos against the Mexicans in the Battle of Copper Pass in 1835. Despite being outnumbered—the Mexicans had one thousand troops to the Navajos' two hundred—Narbona and the Navajos were victorious. However, the Navajos could never obtain a lasting peace with the Mexicans.

conference with a group of Navajo people in the Chuska Mountains of what is now northeastern Arizona. The U.S. officials hoped to explain their government's plans for building forts and peacefully settling in the region.

Unfortunately, the meeting ended abruptly in an outburst of violence. The Navajos attempted to leave the conference after a dispute erupted over a horse that one visitor, a Mexican guide, claimed had been stolen from him. In the ensuing clash, soldiers shot and killed seven Navajos, including an influential leader named Narbona. The survivors told other Navajos about the incident, spreading fear and hatred of the hostile intruders among the tribespeople.

Among those most embittered by Narbona's death was his son-in-law Manuelito, who also was a significant Navajo leader. He and some other prominent Navajos, such as Barboncito, who was both a political and religious leader, grew angry about the Americans' presence on their land. Others, such as Zarcilla Largo and Ganado Mucho, were inclined to accommodate the newcomers and signed a series of treaties with the United States. However, because no one leader had the power to speak for all Navajos, most Navajos had little knowledge of these agreements.

In the early 1850s, the U.S. Army constructed a fort in the heart of Navajo country. Its name, Fort Defiance, suggests the antagonism the Navajos and the U.S. soldiers felt for each other. Relations between the two groups were marked by increasing tension and unease. In July 1858, some Navajos expressed their defiance of the fort's commanding officer by killing his black slave, who was known as Jim. The slave was killed in retribution for the slaughter of Manuelito's cattle that had been grazing on lands that both Manuelito and the U.S. military claimed. The commander, Captain William T.H. Brooks, demanded that the Navajos bring to him the individuals responsible for Jim's murder. Zarcilla Largo offered instead to give Brooks some money as compensation, but the commander refused to accept it. A group of Navajos then brought Brooks the body of a Mexican they had killed and identified him as Jim's murderer. Brooks was not convinced and dispatched troops into the countryside. These forces eventually killed some Navajos who may have known nothing of the original dispute.

At the end of April 1860, Manuelito and Barboncito, determined to eliminate the American presence, led about a thousand warriors in a massive attack on Fort Defiance. The Navajos almost took the fort, but the U.S. troops finally drove the warriors back.

Despite the U.S. Army's victory, skirmishes continued to occur. One of the most tragic took place on September 22, 1861, at Fort Fauntleroy in modern-day New Mexico. In accordance with the terms of a treaty negotiated between the United States and the tribe earlier that year, a group of Navajos traveled to the fort to receive rations of food. As was common on ration days, a series of horse races were held, on which both the Navajos and the U.S. soldiers bet heavily. The Navajos accused the Americans of cheating, but the race judges (all of whom were soldiers) ruled that the charges were unfounded. A dispute followed, and in the confusion the fort's commander, Colonel Manuel Chaves, ordered troops to open fire on the Indians. Twelve women and children were among the Navajos killed.

By the early 1860s, U.S. Army officials were convinced that a major military campaign had to be waged to compel the Navajos to submit to federal authority. This perspective was quickly adopted by Brigadier General James Carleton, who was named commander of the U.S. Army in New Mexico Territory in the fall of 1862.

General Carleton had a problem. The Civil War had broken out a year earlier, but the battles between the Union (the North) and the Confederacy (the South) were being fought almost exclusively east of the Mississippi River. Many U.S. troops stationed in New Mexico Territory were posted to the East for combat duty. As a result, New Mexican settlers were inadequately protected from Indian raids on their livestock. The soldiers who remained also grew increasingly edgy because of their isolation from the Civil War battlefront.

Carleton wanted to let his soldiers exercise their thirst for battle on enemies closer to home—the Navajos and the nearby

(*continued on page 34*)

Manuelito (1818–1894)

Manuelito, who was also known as *Hastiin Ch'iil Hajiin* (Man from Black Weeds), *Ashkii Diyiini* (Holy Boy), and *Nabana' Badané* (Narbona's son-in-law), was born into the Bit'ahni clan (Folded Arms People) near Bear Ears, Utah, around 1818. Manuelito, as the Mexicans named him, is noted for his resistance to Mexican and American invasions of Navajoland, or Dinétah. During his lifetime, *Hastiin Ch'iil Hajiin* was committed to helping the Navajos achieve sovereignty and endeavored to keep Navajo lands.

In following the teachings of his ancestors, Manuelito earned the respect of his people. When he was still a young man, he was noted as a warrior who fought to keep Navajo land. Manuelito's marriage to the daughter of Narbona provided him with the opportunity to learn from the wise leader. In later years, Manuelito married another woman known to Americans as Juanita. In her, he found a valuable companion.

Beginning in the late 1500s, Spaniards and then Mexicans explored the Southwest seeking their fortunes and establishing colonies. Navajos experienced cultural transformations that made them herdsmen and warriors, and they were introduced to the horse, which they used in helping to impede the foreigners' advances. Manuelito witnessed the shifting relationships of peace and conflict between Navajos and Mexicans. In the 1830s, Mexicans rode into Navajoland determined to break Navajo resistance and to capture women and children for the slave trade. Slavery had been practiced in the Southwest, but the slave trade intensified with Euro-American invasions. In a battle at Copper Pass in the Chuska Mountains, warriors led by Narbona and Manuelito successfully defeated the Mexicans. At that time, Manuelito was but a young man.

By the time the United States claimed the Southwest in 1848, Manuelito was noted as a fierce warrior. In 1851, the establishment of Fort Defiance in Navajoland led to a war that ended in the Navajos' defeat. The conflict began over pasture lands that lay outside the newly established fort. In 1858, Captain William T.H. Brooks asserted control of the pastures for use by the U.S. Army. In defiance, Manuelito continued to pasture his livestock on the disputed lands, whereupon Brooks ordered the livestock slaughtered. Soon after, a Navajo killed Brooks' black slave and Brooks demanded that the Navajos produce the murderer. Eventually, the Navajos produced a body, most likely that of a Mexican captive. Enraged at what he considered Navajo arrogance, Brooks called for a war. In 1860, Manuelito and one thousand warriors struck at Fort Defiance but were unable to take the fort.

Shortly thereafter, the Civil War began and the Americans abandoned Fort Defiance. After the Civil War, white settlement again threatened the Navajos. Manuelito led the resistance and urged his people to have courage. Finding Navajos to be obstacles to white expansion, Brigadier General James H. Carleton ordered their removal to a reservation near Fort Sumner, New Mexico, where the Navajos could learn to be civilized.

General Carleton enlisted Indian agent Kit Carson for the campaign against the Navajos. Carson and his men literally scorched Navajoland, destroying cornfields, peach trees, hogans, and livestock. By 1863, destitute Navajos began surrendering to the Americans. As prisoners, they endured a three-hundred-mile journey to the internment camp.

At the prison, Navajos barely survived, but Manuelito vowed to remain free. The U.S. Army wished to either capture or kill Manuelito, but they feared that he served as inspiration to others who eluded their enemy. In 1865, Navajo leaders, including Herrera, met Manuelito and gave him the army's message to surrender. Manuelito refused, declaring that "his mother and his God lived in the West and he would not leave them."

Finally, in 1866, wounded and ill, Manuelito surrendered and was interned at the Bosque Redondo prison. After four years, General Carleton admitted that his plan was not working, and there was talk of returning the Navajos to their former homes. On June 1, 1868, Manuelito and other leaders signed a treaty so they could return to Dinétah. Seventeen days later, more than eight thousand Navajos began the journey home.

Upon return to Dinétah, Manuelito remained an influential leader who articulated his concerns for the return of his people's land. He was appointed head of the first Navajo police force, which kept order on the reservation. In 1874, he traveled with his wife and other Navajo leaders to Washington, D.C., to meet President Ulysses S. Grant. In 1894, Manuelito died from disease and alcoholism, but his widow Juanita and his daughters carried on his messages about the importance of retaining land for the coming generations.

(*continued from page 31*)
Mescalero Apaches. The general's idea of fighting these tribes was quickly approved by the governor of New Mexico Territory. It was also supported by the territory's non-Indian population, which felt vulnerable to Indian attacks.

General Carleton was actually interested in more than simply subduing the Indians. He thought Apache and Navajo country might conceal a wealth of untapped gold ore and other minerals. In order to open the region to full-scale exploration by miners, Carleton hoped to round up the scattered Indian peoples in the region and relocate them to the newly established Fort Sumner on the Pecos River in what is now east-central New Mexico. Confined in a nearby area called the Bosque Redondo (Spanish for "round grove"), they could be overseen easily, and by fewer troops than were needed to police the Indians' traditional territory. Carleton also looked upon the establishment of this *reservation*—the tract of land to which the Indians would be officially restricted—as a means to change the Navajos' and Apaches' traditional ways of life. On the reservation, they would be a captive audience for whites seeking to "civilize" them by preaching Christianity and teaching them other non-Indian values. Held long enough, Carleton reasoned, the Indians might be compelled to *assimilate* into mainstream American society.

To spearhead the initial stages of his program, Carleton selected Kit Carson. A legendary trapper and explorer, Carson had been living in Taos and working as the government's agent, or representative, among the Ute people. He had resigned this post, however, after the Civil War broke out to become a colonel in the New Mexico territorial militia. Carson agreed to help Carleton but not without serious and persistent doubts as to the wisdom of the plan. Nonetheless, Carson and his troops began to battle the Mescalero Apaches. Within six months, the U.S. Army had defeated the tribe and relocated the Mescalero Apache population to Fort Sumner.

In July 1863, Carson and his men journeyed to Fort

Defiance to begin their campaign to subdue the Navajo people. According to Carleton's explicit instructions, all Indians who refused to surrender and relocate ran the risk of being killed. But his message was never communicated to the Navajos. As Carson's men moved into their country, the Navajos fled. They were far more numerous than the Mescalero Apaches, and the rugged terrain increased the challenge of tracking the Indians down. The colonel found himself compelled to take drastic measures to comply with Carleton's ruthless orders.

Stories passed down through generations teach the Navajos of today about this very difficult period in tribal history. The soldiers marched through Canyon de Chelly, in the heart of Navajo country, spoiling wells and burning cornfields and peach orchards. Sometimes they shot Navajos and their live-stock without provocation or even any warning.

The winter of 1863–64 was especially severe. Many Navajos went hungry because the U.S. Army's intrusion made it impossible for them to farm and store food. Some people began to surrender in groups so that they might remain together. These groups gathered at Fort Wingate and nearby Fort Defiance in central New Mexico Territory, the points from which they were to begin their journey to Bosque Redondo. It soon became apparent that there were far more Navajo people than Carleton had anticipated. By the end of 1864, some eight thousand Navajos had surrendered. All would be forced to endure the indignity of the march to Fort Sumner and confinement along the Pecos River.

Tales abound of the suffering and ill-treatment incurred by the Navajos during the *Long Walk*, as the 250-mile march to Bosque Redondo is known today. Navajos who put up any resistance during the Long Walk were physically abused or even shot. Women who gave birth along the way were allowed no time to rest. Old people and children were sorely pressed to keep up with their families.

Some Navajos escaped the hardship of the Long Walk.

Navajo chief Manuelito (shown here in an 1874 photograph) developed an animosity toward the United States after his father-in-law, Narbona, was killed by U.S. troops in 1849. Over the next two decades, the Navajos clashed with U.S. troops before agreeing to sign the Treaty of 1868, which established a reservation for the Navajos in northwestern New Mexico and northeastern Arizona.

Perhaps as many as several thousand fled north and west, into the isolated canyons of what is now northern Arizona or onto Black Mesa, a high, remote plateau within sight of Canyon de Chelly. The great Navajo leaders Manuelito and Barboncito also resisted relocation for some time. Manuelito finally surrendered and arrived at Fort Sumner in 1866. His capitulation prompted Barboncito, Ganado Mucho, and others to turn themselves over to U.S. authorities.

At Fort Sumner, the Navajos suffered greatly from their confinement and their separation from their homeland. The U.S. government had negotiated contracts with non-Indians to provide food rations for the Navajos. However, most of these suppliers were corrupt and made huge profits by giving the Indians meager rations of spoiled food. Many Navajos grew ill with digestive problems. Some also complained that the region's salty water gave them dysentery. The poor soil along the Pecos River produced scanty harvests, which were ravaged by cutworms. And although the U.S. Army had agreed to protect the Navajos at Fort Sumner, Comanches and other tribes raided the outpost.

Evidence mounted that Carleton's experiment had failed. The general increasingly came under criticism, not only from Indians but also from neighboring non-Indians who thought his program was unjust, ill conceived, and poorly managed. Some simply wanted the Navajos removed from the vicinity, believing they could live elsewhere at less expense to the U.S. government. Eventually, Carleton could no longer fend off his critics, and he was relieved of his command in September 1866. In January 1867, the *Bureau of Indian Affairs* (BIA), the federal agency in the Department of the Interior that had been founded in 1824 to manage governmental relations with Indians, took over responsibility for the Navajos' welfare from the U.S. Army.

During the years following the Civil War, the U.S. government reassessed its policy toward all Indians. Officials were especially concerned about dealing with Indians in the West. The number of Americans settling in the region was rising and was expected to increase even more as America's first transcontinental railroad neared completion. To accommodate these settlers, federal policymakers hoped to sign treaties with Indian peoples that would include terms for their confinement on well-defined reservations. To this end, Congress formed the U.S. Indian Peace Commission, a delegation composed of military men and civilians that headed west to negotiate treaties with various tribes. Two of its members, Colonel Samuel F. Tappan and General William Tecumseh Sherman, visited the Navajos at Fort Sumner in the spring of 1868.

At the commissioner's request, the tribe chose ten men—with Barboncito as principal spokesman—to represent the Navajos in these discussions. These representatives argued and pleaded with Tappan and Sherman to allow them to return to their homeland. At a meeting on May 28, Barboncito told the visitors:

> The bringing of us here has caused a great decrease of our numbers—many of us have died, also a great number of our animals. . . . Our Grandfathers had no idea of living in any other country except our own. . . . When the Navajos were first created, four mountains and four rivers were pointed out to us, inside of which we should live; that [which] was to be our country was given to us by the first woman of the Navajos' tribe.

In response, Sherman spoke of the federal policy of relocating, or removing, tribes to Indian Territory, an area in what is now Oklahoma, where many Eastern Indians had been given reservations. Because the Navajos were unhappy in their present home, he asked whether they would come to live in Indian Territory instead. Sherman explained that if they did not want to pursue that option, he would be willing to consider allowing them to return to their homeland. But, he added, if they did go back, they would have to live peacefully within clearly defined boundaries.

Barboncito replied, "I hope to God you will not ask me to go to any other country than my own." The next day at talks to negotiate the Navajos' return home, he said:

Thanks to the persuasiveness of Barboncito (pictured here) and Manuelito, the Navajos were able to return to their homeland (Dinétah) under the terms of the Treaty of 1868. The U.S. government promised the Navajos annuities for a period of ten years as compensation for the land it took from them. In addition, the Navajos were given livestock so they could start their lives anew. After the Navajos signed the treaty, Barboncito was appointed head chief of the tribe by the U.S. government.

After we get back to our country, it will brighten up again and the Navajos will be as happy as the land; black clouds will rise and there will be plenty of rain. Corn will grow in abundance and everything will look happy.

On June 1, 1868, following two more days of meetings, the Navajo representatives signed a treaty with the U.S. government. The document was ratified the following month by the U.S. Senate. The treaty established the initial boundaries of the Navajo Reservation, which included only about one-fourth of

The Treaty of 1868 (Naal Tsoos Sání)

On June 1, 1868, Diné leaders, including Barboncito and Manuelito, signed a treaty with the United States. To the People, the treaty meant that they would return to their homeland after four years of hardship (1864 to 1868) and suffering at Bosque Redondo.

Following U.S. federal Indian policy of either forcing indigenous peoples to relocate to reservations or extermination if they resisted, U.S. Brigadier General James Carleton conceived of an assimilation plan for Navajos: they would be removed to Bosque Redondo, near Fort Sumner in northeastern New Mexico. There, the Diné would become farmers, live in villages, be instructed in Christianity, and send their children to American schools. To force Navajos to surrender, Carleton enlisted Kit Carson, who implemented a "scorch and burn" policy.

In 1863, Carson and his men crisscrossed Dinétah and destroyed cornfields, slaughtered livestock, burned hogans, and cut down peach orchards. By 1864, destitute Navajos turned themselves in at U.S. forts. From the forts, the Navajos were forced to walk 250 miles to Bosque Redondo. Thousands of Navajos made the Long Walk.

The People suffered immensely as Mexican slave raiders followed the prisoners and stole women and children. Soldiers shot the elderly and pregnant women who could not keep up. As the People crossed the Rio Grande, many were swept away by the rapids and drowned. At the prison camp, they endured starvation, poverty, sickness, and cold for four long years. More than 2,500 people died. Manuelito remained free until 1866, when ill and near starvation, he and his band surrendered and made the journey to Bosque Redondo.

The years at the reservation were hard and were filled with suffering for the People. There were not enough rations. Disease and freezing winters took the tribe's traditional territory. The reservation was a rectangular parcel comprising 3.5 million acres in what is now northeastern Arizona and northwestern New Mexico. One article of the treaty required that the United States provide a teacher for every thirty Navajo children between the ages of 6 and 18 "who

their toll. The crops that they planted each year were destroyed by blight and bad weather, while the water was alkaline and made them sick. Some women were forced to prostitute themselves in order to feed their families. And slave raiders always waited outside the reservation to steal women and children.

In 1868, Carleton came under criticism because his plan to assimilate the Navajos was not working. The U.S. government was spending more and more money for the Navajos' upkeep. Finally, federal officials admitted that the assimilation program was a failure. At first, it seemed a possibility that the People could be sent to Indian Territory (present-day Oklahoma). Barboncito, a respected peace chief, spoke to U.S. military leaders on behalf of his people, saying: "I hope to God you will not ask me to go to any other country than my own." Eventually, Barboncito persuaded the military officers to allow his people to return to their beloved homeland.

On June 1, 1868, Navajo leaders signed a peace treaty with the United States. They were promised annuities for a period of ten years as compensation for lands taken. The Diné would receive livestock so they could start their lives again, but the land returned to the People was only a quarter of what they had formerly claimed. The Treaty of 1868 was the last treaty between the Diné and the United States, although a number of executive orders increased the size of Navajo country into the twentieth century.

On June 18, 1868, the People formed a column that stretched at least ten miles long. They were going home. The elders wept in relief. Back in their country, the People reestablished their lives and returned to livestock raising. They remembered their ancestors' teachings. They have not forgotten the Long Walk and the Bosque Redondo. They remember the courage of their leaders during those dark times.

can be induced or compelled to attend school." The U.S. government also pledged to give the Navajo people seeds and farming equipment and to purchase fifteen thousand sheep and goats and five hundred beef cattle for their use. In turn, the Navajos agreed not to oppose the construction of any railroad or roads through the reservation, not to raid non-Indian settlements, and not to block the building of any military posts in their midst.

With the Navajos' return to their ancestral homeland, the people's future suddenly seemed bright once more. Unlike many other tribes, the Navajos had managed to hold on to a significant section of their territory rather than being forced to endure permanent removal to alien ground. Living again within the boundaries of the four sacred mountains gave the Navajos cultural continuity. They knew the land and what it could provide for them in the years to come. If they had been compelled to remain outside of their true home, the history of the Navajos might have been very different. But now, as Barboncito had said, they looked forward to being as happy as the land itself.

4

The Weaving Together of a People

G lad as the Navajos were to leave Fort Sumner in 1868, they faced significant problems upon their return to their homeland. The Long Walk and the years at Bosque Redondo had sapped the strength of many people and disrupted many families. The tribe was allowed to return to only a portion of the land it had occupied in years past. Despite the U.S. government's assurance that the U.S. Army would protect the Navajos, other Indian peoples continued to raid their lands. White settlers also sought the lands at the boundaries of Navajo land, causing conflicts between Navajo sheepherders and white ranchers who both wanted to use public domain lands. Hunger also became a problem when, after a season of bad weather, many of the first crops the Navajos had planted on their reservation yielded small harvests.

But in many ways, the old days were gone, and a new era had begun. Despite their hardships, the people felt fortunate to be living

This delegation of Navajo representatives traveled to Washington, D.C., in 1874 to discuss the provisions of the Treaty of 1868, which called for the U.S. government to supply the Navajos with agricultural implements, seeds for growing crops, livestock, and clothing.

within the four sacred mountains once again. They were also encouraged by the U.S. government's adherence to the terms of the 1868 treaty. In accordance with the agreement, the U.S. government sent a teacher, Charity Gaston, to Fort Defiance to teach a few Navajo children. The government also gave the Navajos the livestock promised in the treaty. The people slowly began to spread across the reservation, feeling more confident about their future.

Ironically, the U.S. government's failed relocation of the Navajos to Bosque Redondo ultimately had some positive results. During this tribulation, the government had treated the Navajos as one people. This changed the Navajos' perception of themselves. Living in independent communities scattered over a vast area, the Navajos had previously had little sense of tribal unity. But now, having experienced the horrors of the Long

Walk, they began to perceive the need to work together to survive and prosper. Thus the foundation of what would eventually be the Navajo Nation was laid in the 1860s.

As their population grew and their sheep multiplied, the Navajos began to find the 3.5-million acre reservation inadequate. In the late nineteenth century, while most Indian tribes were losing land, the Navajos, through their government-appointed Indian agents, began to demand more territory from the U.S. government. Most of the land they sought had been used by them before the Long Walk.

Living in a region then largely neglected by settlers, the Navajos were able to persuade the U.S. government to make, by executive order, three additions to their reservation during the final decades of the 1800s. The first, granted on October 29, 1878, added a narrow rectangular strip of some 960,000 acres next to the western border of their original reservation. On January 6, 1880, a U-shaped area of nearly 100,000 acres to the south was annexed. Finally, in 1884, more than 2 million acres along what is now the Arizona-Utah border were added. This beautiful country had been a place of refuge for many Navajos who had escaped the Long Walk.

In 1882, the federal government, again by executive order, also established a reservation for the Hopi Indians. The Hopis, like the Pueblo and Zuni peoples, were descendants of the Anasazi Indians and had lived in the Southwest for hundreds of years. The Hopis' homes were concentrated on and around three mesas (flat-topped mountains), within their new reservation. The Hopi Reservation boundaries were drawn to include lands the Navajos were already using, and the executive order stipulated that the Hopi land could be occupied by "other Indians as the Secretary of the Interior may see fit to settle thereon." Consequently, the Hopis and Navajos began to share portions of the Hopi Reservation. But this uneasy arrangement did not entirely please either tribe and would result in great problems between the Navajos and the Hopis decades later.

During the late 1800s, the size of the Navajos' herds of live-stock increased dramatically. In 1891, U.S. special agent Dana K. Shipley conducted a survey and concluded that the Navajo people then numbered roughly 17,000. Shipley also concluded that they owned nearly 19,000 horses, 9,000 cattle, 500 mules, and more than 1.5 million sheep. These figures, though probably inflated, clearly indicate the huge growth of the herds. A more reliable source estimates conservatively that the number of sheep and goats soared from perhaps 40,000 in 1868 to nearly 800,000 at the end of the nineteenth century.

Such staggering increases, combined with an expanding land base, suggest that the Navajos were prospering. The tribe was without a doubt staging an impressive comeback from the Bosque Redondo era. However, there was a price to be paid for this headlong development. The mountainous lands of the harsh, dry Southwest had never supported lush greenery. By the late 1800s, the skyrocketing Navajo livestock population had begun to deplete the area's already sparse vegetation. Sheep often eat grass down to its roots.

Cattle and horses, with their great weight and sharp hooves, sometimes trample more grass than they consume. Once vegetation has been ravaged by overgrazing, the exposed land often erodes, as strong winds and flash floods carry away the loose, mineral-rich topsoil, leaving behind only sterile, barren gullies.

The problem of soil erosion loomed even before the turn of the twentieth century. By 1883, Indian agent Dennis Riordan reported to the BIA in Washington, D.C., that the Navajos had "too many sheep" and "an enormous number of useless ponies." He believed that their total sheep herd should be cut by half or more to prevent overgrazing and avert the destruction of their land. Riordan also said that the Navajos had to change their thinking about horses. They did not need so many, he said, but merely liked having great numbers of them. In his opinion, the problem of soil erosion would not be solved until the Navajos changed their attitude about these animals.

The Navajos, however, believed that the solution lay not in reducing their livestock herds but in further increasing their amount of grazing land. Federal policy seemed to encourage this perspective. In the first decade of the twentieth century, four more additions were made to the reservation by executive order. The U.S. government was willing to give this land to the Navajos because northern Arizona's relatively small non-Indian population had little interest in settling this forbidding region. As the Navajos prospered during the late nineteenth and early twentieth centuries, a significant institution began to dot their countryside—the trading post. Usually established and owned by non-Indians, trading posts on the reservation were often the only places of business for many miles around. Naturally, each became a center for local social life. People gathered not only to trade but to visit with one another.

As its name implies, the transactions at a trading post usually involved *barter* rather than money. The Navajos quickly learned to be shrewd bargainers, offering the traders crops, raw wool, or other agrarian products in exchange for goods such as metal pots, fabric, coffee, and flour. Traders sometimes extended credit if the Indian could provide the trader with a pawn—an item left as security. The pawn could be recovered later, when the Navajo had products to pay back the extended credit. If the item was left beyond a specific length of time, however, the trader was entitled to sell it for whatever money it might bring. The Navajos commonly used their jewelry or their intricately woven blankets as pawns. Traders quickly recognized that there was a market among non-Indian customers for these beautiful objects. Soon the traders prized blankets and jewelry not as pawns but as trade items that were as valuable as livestock and agricultural products. In this fashion, traders soon came to have a strong personal interest in the expansion and diversity of the Navajo economy.

Traders such as Lorenzo Hubbell of Ganado, J.B. Moore of Crystal, and Thomas Keam of Keams Canyon encouraged

Navajo women to weave larger blankets that could be used as rugs. The traders then sent out colorful catalogs to merchants in the East that advertised the exceptional creativity of the weavers. With the coming of railroads, such as the Santa Fe line, commerce between the eastern and western United States increased, and there was soon a growing market for Navajo craftwork. Because most Navajos did not speak English and rarely left the reservation, traders became influential interme-diaries between the tribe and non-Indian customers.

Exercising this influence, traders suggested designs they believed would appeal to their customers and discouraged imi-tations of non-Indian rug patterns. Using vertical looms they had adopted from the Pueblos, Navajo women living in differ-ent regions gradually developed distinctive local styles. They also began to use newly available commercial dyes as well as traditional vegetable pigments to color their wool. But even though the weavers saved considerable time by using commer-cial dyes, each rug often took hundreds of hours to make.

Traders also encouraged Navajo men to become master sil-versmiths. Some Navajos had learned silversmithing from Mexicans during the decades before the Long Walk. In the late nineteenth century, trader Lorenzo Hubbell brought Mexican silversmiths to the reservation to teach more Navajo men this skill, and soon these students instructed still more tribesmen. Using Mexican and U.S. coins (such as silver dollars) as raw material, these smiths fashioned intricate belt buckles, buttons, bracelets, rings, earrings, necklaces, horse bridles, and other items.

By the 1890s, Navajo silversmiths had begun setting turquoise into their jewelry. This bluish mineral was mined nearby and brought to the reservation by traders. The juxtapo-sition of turquoise and silver rapidly became a distinctively Navajo look. This jewelry was soon as popular within the tribe as it was with non-Indians.

Traders, though influential, were not the sole non-Indian

Prior to their removal to the reservation, Navajos learned the craft of silversmithing from Mexicans. This artistic endeavor is typically passed down from generation to generation and turquoise is often set into their jewelry. Here a Navajo man is stamping silver conchos on an anvil in this early-twentieth-century photo.

force within the Navajo world at this time. Christian missionaries began to arrive on the reservation in hopes of converting the Indians to their faith. Among the earliest missionaries to come to Navajo country were the Presbyterians, who arrived about 1869 and built a mission in Ganado near Hubbell's trading post. In 1906, they added to this the Ganado Mission School.

Given the proximity of large Mormon settlements in Utah, it is not surprising that the Mormon Church was also a presence on the reservation. As early as the 1870s, some Navajos were baptized by Mormon missionaries. A small Mormon settlement also existed in Moenkopi (near modern-day Tuba City, Arizona), although church members later moved away as the reservation expanded.

The Presbyterians and Mormons were followed in the 1890s by priests of the Franciscan order of the Catholic Church. They located their mission, St. Michaels, near Fort Defiance, about twenty-five miles east of Ganado. The Franciscans subsequently founded St. Michaels Mission School there in 1902. While attempting to convert the Navajos, the priests became interested in their culture. St. Michaels soon emerged as a center for the study of the Navajo language, religion, and way of life.

The Presbyterians and Catholics were soon joined by members of the Methodist and Christian Reformed churches. Both denominations also constructed schools. The Christian Reformed Church established a mission, Rehoboth, in 1898, and built the Rehoboth Mission School in 1903 near the town of Gallup. The Navajo Methodist Mission School, originally situated near Shiprock, was moved to Farmington, New Mexico, east of the reservation, in 1912.

Federal policy during this period encouraged churches to become major participants in Indian education. Mission schools educated many Navajo children who would grow up to become tribal leaders. Although such schools had widely varying views of, and approaches to, Navajo culture, parents who selected them generally did so because of their significant differences from BIA schools. Often the priests at mission schools had put in years of service to the Navajo community, whereas teacher turnover in BIA schools was rapid. Mission schools also were usually (though not invariably) more responsive than BIA schools to parental opinions.

In contrast, the territorial governments of Arizona and New Mexico showed little interest in educating Navajos. However, the federal government continued to fund the Navajo school it had established in the 1860s at Fort Defiance. The BIA founded a few others as well, including one in 1887 at Keams Canyon (attended by both Navajo and Hopi pupils) and another in 1895 at Tohatchi. A small number of Navajo students attended off-reservation federal boarding schools, such as those founded at Albuquerque in 1886, at Santa Fe in 1890, and at Phoenix in 1891. A few (usually older) students went to the leading federal Indian schools of the day—Haskell Institute in Lawrence, Kansas, and Carlisle Indian Industrial School in Carlisle, Pennsylvania.

Most public education of Indians at this time aimed to assimilate students into mainstream American society. Teachers taught in English and generally discouraged or even prohibited use of the Navajo language. Courses emphasized non-Indian values, priorities, and needs.

It is scarcely surprising that many Navajo parents, especially those who followed tribal traditions closely, opposed an educational program that tried to make their children part of an alien society. Moreover, they often needed their children to assist with herding the sheep and other necessary work at home. Therefore, most Navajo children either did not attend school or went for only a short time. Sometimes parents chose one child in their family to attend school while his or her siblings worked. Many non-Indian parents across the United States did likewise during this era, when even a high school education was out of reach for most children.

Many angry confrontations occurred when agents or school truant officers attempted to compel Navajo children to attend school. Parents often barred the doorway of their hogan and refused to let these officials take their children. On one occasion in 1893, Dana K. Shipley tried to seize children against their will and force them to attend the Fort Defiance boarding school many miles away. A Navajo leader named Black Horse then apprehended Shipley. The agent barely escaped serious injury from furious parents.

However the Navajos may have felt about the world outside the reservation, that world encroached increasingly upon their own. In the early 1900s, geological surveys revealed the possible presence of oil on Navajo land. In 1921, after a major oil discovery was made in northwestern New Mexico, the Midwest Refining Company gained permission from the BIA to negotiate with the Navajos for the right to drill on the reservation. Company officials were eager to begin talks but were hindered by one problem: They had no idea with whom they were to negotiate. The Navajo Reservation was a very large area with a substantial population. The Navajos had only recently begun to think of themselves as one people, and the old spirit of local independence had not entirely disappeared. Who dared speak for all the Navajos?

By the 1920s, the BIA had divided the Navajo Reservation into six administrative areas. These were called the Southern, Western, San Juan (Northern), Pueblo Bonito (Eastern), Leupp, and Moqui jurisdictions. (The Moqui Jurisdiction would later become the Hopi Indian Agency.) The BIA assigned one agent to each division. When an important problem arose, an agent might call together certain Navajos in his division for a special meeting. The Navajo people had no interdivision council, however.

Potential oil income created a number of questions that the Navajos needed a central governing body to solve. For example, the Midwest Refining Company planned to drill near Shiprock, so the people living there would be more inconvenienced by the venture. Yet the oil money might, theoretically, be used to benefit Navajos in all areas. Somehow the tribe had to determine who should reap the rewards of the business deal when the drawbacks would be felt by only one portion of the population.

Initially, the Navajos of the Shiprock area met in informal councils to consider possible leases. But they did not act quickly enough to satisfy either the BIA or the Midwest Refining Company. In 1922, the BIA selected prominent Navajo leaders Chee Dodge, Charlie Mitchell, and Dugal Chee Bekis to serve as a business council for the whole reservation. Dodge, the son of a Navajo mother and a Mexican father, was especially respected as an educated businessman, community leader, orator, and interpreter. All three leaders served their people thoughtfully. But they were not elected representatives, and the arrangement was clearly unsatisfactory in the long run.

The following year, a tribal council was established according to rules set forth by the BIA. The council was to be composed of twelve delegates and twelve alternates elected by the Navajo people. The size of the population of each division would determine how many representatives it could send to the council. The area around Shiprock (the San Juan jurisdiction) could have three delegates, and that around Fort Defiance (the Southern Jurisdiction) four, because these divisions included the largest number of people. The people of each division on the reservation then met and elected twelve councilmen whose names reflected the diversity of the Navajo population: George Bancroft, Todachene Bardony, Becenti Bega, Hosteen Begoiden Bega, Deshna Cahcheschillige, Hosteen Yazzie Jesus, Robert Martin, Jacob Morgan, Hosteen Nez, Hosteen Usahelin, Louis Watchman, and Zagenitzo. Even though the organization had been imposed upon the Navajos, who had mixed feelings about its very existence, the formation of the council was undeniably a significant step in the tribe's political unification.

The new Navajo Tribal Council held its first meeting on July 7, 1923, in Toadlena, New Mexico, and elected Chee Dodge as its chairman. The councilmen would not have long to wait before confronting some difficult questions.

5

The Time of Livestock Reduction

The 1920s were the start of a period of intense political, social, and economic transition for the Navajo people. Although the political changes were most obvious and immediate, the social and economic changes that began at this time would have an equally important effect on the tribe's immediate future.

During the 1920s, the newly formed Navajo Tribal Council annually held only one regular session, lasting but a few days. The council's primary business was to decide whether to lease land to oil companies that wanted to drill on the reservation. The council members studied each proposed lease carefully. As they became more experienced in these negotiations, they increasingly demanded that their people receive a fair royalty, or percentage, of the oil companies' profits.

After several leases were approved, oilmen began to drill exploratory wells, a number of which proved to be dry holes—sites

Navajo wool woven blanket, circa 1870–1885, Colorado Historical Society, Denver, Colorado. By the late 1800s, blankets and rugs had become an essential part of the Navajos' economy—they were prized by Arizona traders, who promoted the craftsmanship to merchants in the East.

Navajo wool rug with diamond pattern, circa 1890–1920, Colorado Historical Society, Denver, Colorado. By the late 1800s, Navajo women created their own local styles and used commercial dyes to color the wool of their rugs, which sometimes took hundreds of hours to make.

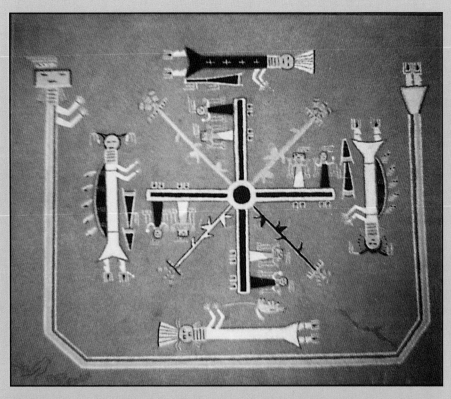

Navajo sand-painting with abstract figures and geometric patterns, Decorative and Fine Arts Department, Colorado Historical Society, Denver, Colorado. Also called drypaintings, these images are made with dry pigments, such as sand and corn pollen, and are used in Navajo curative ceremonies.

Over the years, silver has become synonymous with Navajo jewelry. Shown here is a silver step design pin and earrings that are inset with lapis (a semiprecious stone) squares and beadwork.

This rug, which is on display at the Smithsonian American Art Museum, in Washington, D.C., was made by Navajo weaver Louise Nez. Much of Nez's work depicts her early life on the Navajo Reservation.

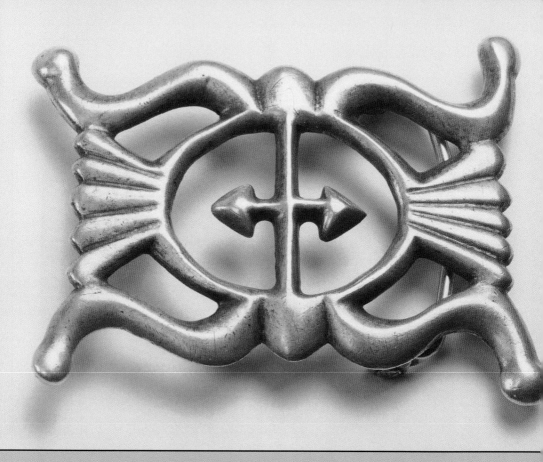

Twentieth-century Navajo sandcast silver belt buckle. After the Navajos were forced onto the reservation in the late nineteenth century, they often became silversmiths and used Mexican and U.S. coins to create intricate belt buckles, bracelets, and necklaces, among other items.

By the 1890s, Navajo silversmiths had begun setting turquoise into their jewelry, which quickly became a Navajo trademark. This contemporary chip inlay bola tie was made by a Navajo silversmith in the 1960s and includes turquoise, coral, and jet.

Squash blossom necklaces, which are made of silver and turquoise, often include an inverted crescent pendant, or Naja—a design that is included in many Navajo jewelry pieces.

Pictured here are members of the Navajo Tribal Council: Marcus Kanuho (vice-chairman, 1932–36), Deshna Clah Cheschillige (chairman, 1928–32), Henry Chee Dodge (founding chairman 1922–28), Thomas Dodge (chairman, 1932–36), and Henry Taliman, Sr. (chairman, 1937–38). The Navajo Tribal Council was established in 1923 and is composed of twelve delegates and twelve alternates elected by the Navajo people.

that yielded no oil. The small amount of oil obtained from the few producing wells was a disappointment to the oilmen and the Navajos alike. The royalty money that trickled into the tribal treasury was also less than overwhelming. The companies soon discovered oil in other regions of the Southwest, and by the end of the decade, most oilmen had turned their attention away from the Navajo Reservation.

Although unsuccessful, the search for oil on the reservation had had the positive effect of forcing the creation of the council, which continued to be responsible for the tribe's well-being. And the council members took their job seriously. Rather than deciding to divide the relatively small oil revenue among the Navajos, giving each person a small sum of money, the council put the entire amount into a general tribal fund to benefit the Navajos as a whole. The sum was initially used as an emergency relief fund to help those stricken by natural disasters such as severe droughts. The council's decision to use the oil money to help the tribe as a group was in keeping with traditional Navajo values. It would also serve as an important precedent later, when the council would have to deal with much larger sums.

Although the council was effective at solving problems that involved the entire tribe, it was not equipped to make decisions regarding all the many day-to-day local concerns of the Navajos. Another type of political organization was needed to deal appropriately with neighborhood problems. In 1927, John Hunter, the agent of one of the reservation's six divisions, devised such organizations within his jurisdiction. Hunter organized communities into *chapters*. The people in each chapter elected officers, who held meetings to discuss local issues.

The other divisions of the Navajo Reservation quickly adopted the chapter system. It worked because it dealt with matters best handled locally. For example, two families might disagree over who had the right to graze sheep on a certain piece of land and ask their chapter leaders to settle the dispute. The Navajo people had for generations resolved this type of disagreement by discussing it with local leaders. The new procedure therefore simply formalized an existing tradition. An extra benefit was that the tribal council could meet with chapter representatives to learn about local issues and thereby keep in touch with common concerns. Eventually, nearly one hundred chapters existed across the reservation. They were formed around the widely scattered Navajo communities and varied in size, but each usually comprised at least a few hundred people.

Despite the chapter system's success, chapter councils did not officially become part of the tribal government for many years. The same is true of two other branches of the Navajo government: its police force and court system. A Navajo court system had been authorized by the federal government in 1883 but was not instituted until 1891. Informal police forces had formed on occasion for specific tasks, such as retrieving stolen cattle, but a permanent corps of police developed only in the 1880s.

Such gradual and informal changes in Navajo society were, however, soon to be rushed under federal pressure, primarily because of the soil erosion issue. In 1928, Assistant Commissioner of Indian Affairs E.B. Meritt journeyed from Washington, D.C., to Leupp, Arizona, to tell Navajo councilmen that the federal government wanted the people eventually to limit the number of their sheep, horses, goats, and cattle. Two years later, a BIA forester, William Zeh, completed a survey of Navajo lands and arrived at discouraging conclusions. Zeh called the Navajo range "deteriorating" and noted that one of the main reasons for this situation was the region's inadequate water supply. Herds had to travel long distances to get water, and the large numbers of livestock overgrazed the sparse vegetation during their journey. As a result, the region suffered further soil erosion.

In February 1931, BIA officials yet again met among themselves to discuss the growing problem. They concluded that Navajo herds would have to be reduced in number if the reservation land were ever to improve. The officials assumed that if the Navajo people could be made to understand the gravity of their predicament, they would willingly adopt stern measures.

The Navajos, however, saw their situation differently. Traders had long encouraged them to expand their flocks, and the federal government had over the years added a good deal of land to the reservation. The Navajos believed that if the U.S. government would only continue to increase their territory, these additions—along with more rain—would solve the problem perceived by the white men. A prolonged period of drought had in fact added to the soil erosion problem, but there was an element of wishful thinking in the Navajos' expectations of greater rainfall.

A changing political situation outside the reservation also made enlarging the reservation difficult. The growing non-Indian population of Arizona and New Mexico, which had become states in 1912, had elected congressmen and senators who clamored against making public property part of Navajo country. They instead wanted public lands and money devoted to such projects as Boulder Dam, then under construction on the Colorado River in northwestern Arizona. The dam, later renamed Hoover Dam after President Herbert Hoover, would become on its completion in 1936 one of the largest in the world, providing flood control, irrigation, and electric power to the entire southwestern United States.

In the fall of 1932, following the onset of a severe economic depression throughout the United States, Franklin D. Roosevelt succeeded Hoover as president. Roosevelt appointed John Collier as his new commissioner of Indian affairs. Collier had become fascinated with Indian life while traveling through the Southwest. He became an impartial advocate of Indian rights during the 1920s, when he joined the Navajos' neighbors, the Pueblos, in their fight against a congressional bill that sought to diminish their territory. He had come to admire the Pueblos' traditional emphasis on community and, as commissioner of Indian affairs, wanted to help Indian people across the country achieve a brighter future. The programs he introduced at the BIA recognized the diversity of Indian cultures and supported the Indians' right to be consulted in shaping federal Indian policy.

When Collier heard of the soil erosion in Navajo country and the tribe's need for more land, he became determined to use his position to help them. But he knew little about the Navajos' history and society, especially about the importance of livestock in their culture. Because of his lack of understanding of their way of life, Collier soon antagonized the Navajos, who came to regard this man as an enemy.

Collier believed that to save their ranges, the Navajos should be granted more land and, at the same time, cut back on their livestock. He told tribal council members that if they would agree to livestock reduction, he would be able to get them additional territory, along with local schools, water development, and federal jobs that were part of Roosevelt's New Deal program to revive the national economy. Collier was able to obtain congressional approval for two very small additions to the reservation on its northern and western boundaries and a larger extension on its southern border. But strong opposition by congressmen from New Mexico blocked any chance of expansion to the east. Although the actions of Congress were clearly beyond Collier's control, the Navajos felt he had failed to meet his part of the bargain when their reservation was not significantly enlarged.

Collier, however, felt he was doing his best and, moreover, doing the right thing by compelling the Navajos to reduce their livestock. Factors other than land conservation influenced the commissioner's actions. The workability of Boulder Dam appeared endangered by the vast amount of silt that continued to erode from Navajo lands and run off into the Colorado River. Also, with the national economy so depressed, there was little if any demand on the free market for Navajo livestock. If the tribe was to make it through these difficult times, Collier concluded, he had no choice but to override the Navajos' objections to his course of action.

From about 1933 to 1935, livestock reduction was largely voluntary. Collier used funds from the Federal Emergency Relief Administration to purchase Navajo sheep and goats, which were then shipped off to be used to feed impoverished people elsewhere in the country. In an effort to cooperate, the Navajo Tribal Council voted that everyone in the tribe should accept a flat 10 percent reduction in their herds. But this cut proved to be only the first step in a drastic program that would last for more than a decade and affect the Navajos' entire way of life.

In 1933, the Bureau of Indian Affairs instituted a policy of livestock reduction among the Navajos because overgrazing was damaging Navajo land. Under its terms, John Collier, commissioner of the BIA, promised the Navajos that they would be granted more land if they reduced the size of their horse, sheep, and goat herds. Although Collier initially attempted to carry out this policy with Navajo cooperation, range riders were eventually used to round up livestock (like the horses shown here) and either shipped them off to be slaughtered or killed them on-site.

Even today, the Navajos remember the years of livestock reduction with bitterness. The memories are fresh and strong because the people have passed the stories down from one generation to the next. The stories tell of sheep being forcibly taken from their owners, driven over the next hill or into the next valley, and then shot and left to rot. Beloved horses were also taken away and shot. Some Navajos went to jail for refusing to round up livestock or for fighting the agents who carried out the reduction program.

The Navajos were always paid at least a small amount for the livestock seized from them. But they resented the loss of their livestock—especially of their sheep—because they saw it as an attack not only upon their means of support but upon their very culture. Sheep were the traditional payment given to a singer for presiding over a sacred ceremony. The animals were also needed to feed visiting relatives and neighbors. Perhaps most important, Navajo children learned traditional tribal values and responsibilities by helping to care for their family's sheep herd. Without sheep, how could a child learn what it was to be a member of the people?

Not only the act of livestock reduction but the way in which it was done embittered the Navajos. After 1936, the U.S. government seemed to approach the program as a crusade to be carried out with a vengeance. Agents started forcibly taking away livestock without any explanation to the animals' owners. The U.S. government did dispatch employees to the reservation to help the Navajos and to try to persuade them to cooperate. But the agents performed their task too quickly and with too little sensitivity. The Navajo people could not see why they should surrender their precious sheep herds, built up over generations, to this man they had never met, this John Collier.

A resistance movement soon arose under the leadership of Jacob Morgan, a spokesman for the Navajos in the northern area of the reservation, near Shiprock. The people from this portion of the reservation expressed their anger at John Collier by voting overwhelmingly against reorganizing their tribal government according to the provisions of the *Indian Reorganization Act* (IRA) of 1934. This ground-breaking legislation radically changed federal Indian policy and had been strongly supported by Collier. Among the IRA's aims were the end of unregulated sale of Indian land, the appropriation of federal funds to buy more land for tribes, and the establishment of a system of federal loans for tribal economic development. Perhaps most important, it allowed tribes, if they desired, to adopt formal constitutions and thereby give their tribal governments more legitimacy in their dealings with the

(*continued on page 64*)

The Effects of Livestock Reduction on the Navajos

The Holy People gifted the Diné with sheep. For the Diné, sheep were at the center of life and taught values based on K'e—the principles of maintaining kinship. Ownership taught industry, responsibility, and trust. Caring for livestock required the family's cooperation, and sheep were a sign of status and general well-being. When Blessingways were performed to reaffirm kin and family ties, sheep were brought into the hogan to receive their blessings.

When the Diné returned to their homeland in 1868, they took with them the few remaining livestock in their care. Under the agreements of the Treaty of 1868, the Diné received fifteen thousand sheep and five hundred heads of cattle. Back in their homeland, many families returned to former residences and reestablished a livelihood based on pastoralism. In contrast to other Native peoples who, with military defeat and relocation from their lands, experienced population decrease and some erosion of cultural practices, the Diné steadily increased their own population, as well as that of their livestock. Further, their way of life, where they lived in kin networks miles from each other, allowed for their cultural practices to thrive. Taking care of livestock meant that the Navajos constantly had to search for new grazing lands, going beyond the reservation borders onto public domain—lands that they had formerly claimed for their use prior to 1868.

By the 1880s, Indian agent Dennis Riordan reported an increase in Navajo livestock and called for reduction by at least one-half to two-thirds. Severe drought from 1898 through 1904, combined with growing numbers of livestock took a toll on the land. Range land was sparse of grass, water holes were drying up, and the sheep and goats appeared thin. In 1933, federal officials reported that the Navajos owned more than 1 million head of livestock, the majority being sheep and goats. And about 45 percent of the topsoil had blown away as a result of overgrazing.

To better understand the deteriorating environmental conditions that were attributed to Navajo livestock and grazing practices, forest ranger William Zeh documented damage to the land. The Zeh Report recommended water sources development, rodent control, the elimination of surplus horses, and sheep and goat reduction. Further, other observers noted that soil erosion on Navajo land caused silt to blow into nearby Hoover Dam and Lake Powell.

In 1933, under BIA Commissioner John Collier, the Navajos were ordered to reduce their herd by 45 percent by the 1950s. Countering prevailing attitudes toward Native peoples of the period, Collier embraced cultural pluralism and encouraged Native peoples to retain their cultural practices and languages. However, because of his insistence that Navajos reduce their livestock, he was not well regarded or trusted. Instead, as Howard Gorman noted, "What John Collier did in livestock reduction is something the people will never forget." Collier's manner of forcing livestock reduction would have long-term ramifications and leave a bitter legacy that reinforced Navajo distrust of the federal government.

Initially, Collier attempted to reduce herds with Navajo cooperation. He called for voluntary reduction, with 10 percent across-the-board cuts where larger owners could cull weak sheep. Owners were compensated by the U.S. government, which donated the sheep and goats to those affected by the Great Depression. Unfortunately, reduction did not occur as Collier had hoped. By 1937, hired range riders were taking animals by force. Because the animals were far from slaughtering houses or places where they could be shipped to factories for processing, the animals were slaughtered and their carcasses left to rot. Resisting Navajos were threatened with jail time and BIA employees were told not to protest. Eventually, by the 1950s, livestock was reduced and Navajos showed their deep disapproval in a number of ways.

When Collier approached the Navajos with his plans for livestock reduction, he promised them additional land along the eastern border of their reservation. He also encouraged Navajo leaders to adopt the Indian Reorganization Act, which would allow them to reorganize under their own constitution, bring about more political and economic autonomy, and make them eligible for certain federal loans. Embittered Navajos rejected the IRA, to Collier's disappointment.

The livestock reduction program created eighteen land management districts and a livestock permit system that is still in use today. It also made more pronounced systemic poverty where some families were left destitute after they lost their livestock. In response, Navajos left their homes to enter the off-reservation wage economy and also adopted a new religion on Navajo land. Bereft and despairing, many Navajos sought assistance in the peyote religion, which today has become the Native American Church.

(*continued from page 61*)

BIA. Many Navajos, including Chee Dodge, wanted their people to have a constitution because they wanted a stronger tribal council. But the very fact that Collier supported the IRA made many others suspicious. When the entire tribe's vote was counted, the Navajos had rejected the IRA's provisions. To this day, the Navajos do not have a constitution, though some people have recently argued the need for one to increase federal government responsiveness and ensure the rights of Navajo individuals.

Other programs supported by Collier met with Navajo opposition for the same reason: guilt by association. The commissioner had been a severe critic of the off-reservation Indian boarding schools that had been operated by the federal government for more than fifty years. These institutions separated children not only from their parents but also from their culture. Collier instead favored day schools, from which children could return to their family each evening. He also wanted day schools to educate Indian students about their history and traditions, including their native language.

Many day schools were established in the 1930s on the Navajo Reservation. Some of the teaching methods advocated by Collier would later be accepted by the Navajo people. Yet when the schools first opened, many Navajos spoke out against them. They were suspicious because day schools were a new idea and because they were linked with the unpopular John Collier.

During the late 1930s, the Navajo government underwent a number of changes at the direction of the BIA. In 1935, the six administrative divisions of the reservation were combined into a single agency, with its headquarters at Window Rock, Arizona. This agency was overseen by a single agent. The first to hold the office was E. Reesman Fryer, who was especially interested in carrying out the BIA's program for soil erosion control.

In 1938, the U.S. secretary of the interior established new regulations for the Navajo Tribal Council itself. Henceforth, a much larger number of delegates (initially 74, but increasing with the population) were to be elected for four-year terms by popular vote of the Navajo people. Other positions included a tribal chairman, a vice-chairman, and an executive committee chosen by the delegates.

As the tribal government changed, so, too, did the Navajo economy under the rigors of livestock reduction. With many people's herds now radically diminished, they could no longer depend upon raising livestock for their livelihood. The BIA tried to compensate by making federal public-works jobs available, but those Navajos who had suffered most from the reduction program were not always the ones who found work.

In some ways, the warnings of Chee Dodge to the U.S. Senate Committee on Indian Affairs seemed to have been accurate. Dodge had cautioned the committee during a public hearing in 1936:

> You take sheep away from a Navajo, that's all he knows. He isn't going to farm or anything like that; you might give a few acres to the poor ones, but stock-raising is in their heart. That's their work. If you keep on cutting down sheep, after a while the government will have to feed these people, give them rations; you know what that will cost.

Once reduction had fully taken effect on the reservation, a great many Navajos continued to live off the land, but gradually more began to seek work for wages in the small towns on the reservation and in the larger cities just beyond the borders of Navajo country. Some found jobs in railroad construction. Others worked as domestic servants, restaurant workers, or in similar service positions. At first, the number of wageworkers was merely a trickle, but job seeking would become increasingly common by the late 1940s.

Such economic changes naturally had an impact on Navajo society. Extended families were affected by the absence of family members working off the reservation. This in turn disrupted the traditional way of rearing children, as well as customary relations among family members. The inability of traditional religious leaders to restore the balance of the Navajo world led some Navajos to consider alternatives or additions to their old religious practices. Some became more active within the various Christian churches. Others turned to a faith already established among many other tribes, the *Native American Church.*

The Native American Church combines elements of Christianity with rituals of traditional Indian religions. The most controversial aspect of the church—especially among the Navajos of the 1940s—was its ritual use of the peyote button, an outgrowth of the mescal cactus native to Mexico and the Southwest. Peyote buttons contain the drug mescaline and other substances that commonly induce hallucinations when ingested. For members of the Native American Church, the chewing of peyote buttons during religious rites is a means of communicating with God, and participation in the church helps them reaffirm their cultural identity and deal with life's difficulties. Some Navajos, however, opposed the Native American Church because its beliefs and practices differed from the tribe's traditions. In 1940, the Navajo Tribal Council passed a resolution outlawing the use or possession of *peyote*, and tribal police sometimes arrested church members on such charges.

Although some members of the council were strongly criticized for their willingness to sanction the arrest of fellow tribe members and for their apparent cooperation in the livestock reduction program, the council became increasingly important throughout the 1930s. Like the Long Walk nearly eighty years earlier, the calamity of the reduction program had brought the Navajos together. To avoid future persecution, the Navajos now understood that they had to create a strong, independent government of their own—one that would benefit the people. As they mulled over how to proceed, their lives were suddenly and dramatically altered by the United States' involvement in World War II.

6

The Modern Navajo Era Begins

Some non-Indian Americans are surprised to learn that the Navajos played a vital role in helping the United States emerge victorious in World War II. They cannot understand why so many Navajos enlisted and fought for the United States, when Indians had so often been mistreated by the government and disparaged by non-Indian individuals. Certainly the era of livestock reduction had embittered many Navajos toward federal authority. Yet an impressive number saw themselves as both Navajo and American and wanted to become involved in the war effort. When the Japanese bombed Pearl Harbor, Hawaii, in December 1941, these Navajos felt it was their country that had been attacked and wanted to defend it.

In the Pacific theater of military operations, Navajo soldiers contributed a remarkable chapter to their people's proud history. At the battlefront, the U.S. armed forces needed a code to send messages that the Japanese could not easily decipher. Philip Johnston, the son

In March 1989, a bronze statue was erected in Phoenix, Arizona, to honor the Navajo Code Talkers who served in the U.S. Marines during World War II. Shown here is Dr. Samuel Billison, then-president of the Navajo Code Talkers' Association, addressing an audience during the dedication of the statue. Billison passed away in November 2004, at the age of seventy-eight.

of a missionary who had lived in Navajo country, came up with a plan. He suggested that the Navajo language serve as the basis for a code. The Marine Corps approved his idea and recruited several hundred Navajo men, who became known as the Navajo *Code Talkers.* (*continued on page 72*)

The Code Talkers: "Bizaa yee nidaaz'baa" (They Fought the Enemy with Their Language)

When Japan bombed Pearl Harbor on December 7, 1941, like many other Americans, Navajos were quick to join the fight to defend their country. More than 3,600 Navajos enlisted in the U.S. armed forces when President Franklin D. Roosevelt declared war on Japan and its allies. Twelve Navajo women also enlisted in the Army Air Corps. The Japanese army seemed invincible, claiming territories in the Philippines, Southeast Asia, and Indonesia. The Japanese were also adept at breaking secret codes, much to the dismay of the United States.

Philip Johnston, a civil engineer and the son of missionaries who had lived on the Navajo Reservation, learned about the need to develop a code the Japanese could not decipher. Knowing that few outside of Arizona and New Mexico had information about the Navajo language and its intricacies, Johnston approached the marines at Camp Elliott, California, to share his plan to develop a code using the Navajo language. Although the marines were skeptical, they allowed Johnston and a few Navajos to demonstrate how the code worked. Impressed with the ability of the Navajos to relay messages in their language and then translate into English, the marine recruiters went to Navajoland to enlist the first Code Talkers for service.

The first twenty-nine Navajo recruits were sent to Camp Elliott in April 1942. They joined the 382nd Platoon, Fourth Marine Division. After successfully completing boot camp, they were trained in communications: The men studied Morse code, semaphore signals, techniques of military message writing, wire laying, pole climbing, and other communication procedures. The Navajo soldiers employed Diné words for military terms, foreign countries, and other topics. A bomber plane was *jeeshóó'* (buzzard), a submarine became *beeshlóó'* (iron fish), and a battleship became *lóótsoh* (whale). Each letter of the English alphabet underwent a transformation. In the code, *wólachíí'* (ant) stood for "a." *Shash* (bear) stood for "b." And *mosí* (cat) stood for "c."

After eight weeks of basic training, the Navajo men were sent overseas, where they played an important role in reclaiming territories that Japan held. Joining the initial twenty-nine recruits were more than four hundred Navajo men. They played key roles at Guadalcanal, Tarawa, Peleiu, and Iwo Jima. During the first forty-eight hours at Iwo Jima, the Code Talkers sent eight hundred messages without error. One major commented, "Without the Code Talkers, the Marines would never have taken Iwo Jima."

After World War II ended, the United States kept the code secret and the Code Talkers returned to civilian life with virtually no recognition for the role they played in helping the United States win the war against Japan. At home, they continued to experience discrimination and racism—Navajos were not allowed to vote in New Mexico and Arizona until 1948.

Finally, after decades of silence, the Code Talkers were recognized for their patriotism. In 1968, the U.S. Department of Defense declassified the Navajo code. At the Fourth Marine Division's reunion in 1969, the marines made the Code Talkers their honored guests. In 1976, a television station in Phoenix, Arizona, helped raise money to send the Code Talkers to Washington, D.C., where they proudly marched in the nation's Bicentennial parade. In 1982, the Senate passed a resolution and President Ronald Reagan declared August 14 as "National Navajo Code Talkers Day." A Code Talkers Association was formed and today the members represent the Navajo Nation in ceremonies and parades throughout the country.

On July 26, 2001, four of the surviving Code Talkers from the original twenty-nine and families of the other twenty-five, traveled to Washington, D.C., to receive the Congressional Gold Medal, the highest civilian award Congress can bestow. John Brown, Jr., Chester Nez, Lloyd Oliver, and Allen Dale June traveled with their families to receive recognition for their loyalty to the United States. Joe Palmer was unable to attend the ceremony but was represented by his son.

President George W. Bush said, "Today, we honor twenty-nine Native Americans who, in a desperate hour, gave their country a service only they could give. Today we give these exceptional Marines the recognition they earned so long ago."* In a separate ceremony, the other Code Talkers were awarded the Silver Congressional Medal.

In paying tribute to the Code Talkers, the United States honored the Navajo men's courage, intelligence, and perseverance, and their defense of their country.

* The full press release can be found at *http://www.congressionalgoldmedal.com/NavajoCodeTalkerslg.htm*

(*continued from page 69*)

The Code Talkers proved very effective at their job. When the U.S. Marines landed on Japanese-held islands, such as Iwo Jima, Guam, and Tarawa, the Code Talkers were in the front lines, establishing communication posts. Using code words and phrases (such as "sparrow hawk" for "dive bomber"), they could converse much more rapidly than anyone using an invented language, and their Japanese adversaries never cracked the complex Navajo code.

Navajo men also fought in Europe against German and Italian forces, and Navajo women served in the Women's Army Corps. Before leaving home to join the military, Navajo men and women commonly took part in a variation of the ancient Blessingway ceremonies used to safeguard departing warriors. After they returned home, they took part in other ceremonies to restore hózhó lost through their wartime experiences and their contact with other cultures. Some veterans who had seen combat partook in a ceremony called the Enemyway, devised to protect warriors from the spirits of their slain enemies.

To this day, older Navajos remember the World War II era with great emotion. More than 3,600 served in the various branches of the military, and for many, the war was their first exposure to the world outside the reservation. To the generation that lived through that time, the Code Talkers came to symbolize the Navajo role in America's ordeal and ultimate triumph, and they were singled out for honors by both fellow Navajos and non-Indians. In 1989, for example, a large statue of a Code Talker was erected in Phoenix, Arizona.

On the reservation, money sent home by Navajo servicemen temporarily helped the tribe's suffering economy. Some Navajo civilians found work off the reservation as factory workers and as field hands harvesting sugar beets, which were used as a substitute for imported cane sugar during the war. People also continued to make their living by traditional means, such as weaving, silversmithing, and farming. Livestock raising, however, was in decline. The reduction program was

Two Navajo Code Talkers send a message during the Battle of Bougainville in November 1943. Navajos played an important role in the U.S. war effort during World War II—more than 3,600 Navajos enlisted in the U.S. armed forces.

carried out through the mid-1940s. After the program had been concluded, U.S. government officials collected statistics that showed that the average weight and wool production of Navajo sheep had increased. To support this conclusion, they had photographs of Navajo sheep before and after the program, observing how much healthier the animals in the latter appeared. The Navajos, of course, did not see it this way.

At the end of the war, the return of thousands of unemployed veterans to the reservation caused an economic crisis. It was impossible for the Navajos to prosper with a livestock-based economy, yet well-paid jobs off the reservation were out of reach to most because of their limited command of English and lack of education. The veterans, who had been immersed in the ways of the outside world, were convinced that Navajo society had to learn for its own good to deal more effectively with the non-Indian populace.

In addition to all these concerns, the Navajos and other groups were being confronted with a changing attitude among non-Indians toward traditional Indian ways of life. All Americans had worked together to win the war, putting differences aside for a common cause. Because Indians had played such a valiant role in achieving victory, many non-Indians concluded that they deserved to be treated just like all other Americans. They argued that Indian communities should no longer be separated or segregated from the majority of the population.

This sentiment inspired a new federal Indian policy known as *Termination*. This policy sought to terminate, or end, the federal government's financial responsibilities to tribes and gradually to withdraw its special protection of reservation lands. The individual state governments would then assume much of the responsibility for the well-being of the Indians within their boundaries. Advocates of Termination felt it would "free" Indians to join mainstream American society.

But most Indians, including the Navajos, opposed Termination, regarding it not as a reward but as a threat. They did not want to be treated just like everyone else because they were *not* just like everyone else. They argued that Indians, as the original inhabitants of North America, had a unique history. Their ancestors had signed treaties and agreements with the federal government, and therefore they were entitled to the unique legal status that these treaties granted them. Although tribes were not always pleased with the way in which the federal government acted toward them, they were even warier of state governments, most of which in the past had shown little interest in the Indians.

One of the earliest instruments of Termination policy was the *Indian Claims Commission* (ICC), which was authorized by

Congress in 1946. The ICC established a temporary federal court in which tribes could sue the federal government for lost land and other damages. Resolution of, and compensation for, these claims was to be a preliminary step in ending the federal government's financial obligation to Indian groups.

Before the Navajos could sue the U.S. government, they needed legal assistance, and they had never before employed a lawyer or law firm to represent them. One of the first acts of Tribal Chairman Sam Ahkeah, who was elected in 1946, was to hire Norman Littell, a former U.S. assistant attorney general. Littell took on the job as the Navajos' attorney in addition to his partnership in a Washington, D.C., law firm.

Littell was a bright and forceful man who left a major imprint on the Navajo people. During the nearly twenty years Littell acted as their lawyer, he encouraged the Navajos to develop their political institutions and generally look out for their own economic and legal interests. He advised the tribal council, represented the Navajos in various cases, and was a vital force in the tribal capital of Window Rock, Arizona, for a generation. During Littell's years as the Navajos' attorney, he encouraged the tribal council to meet more often and take a more aggressive stance toward non-Indian-owned businesses on the reservations.

In 1947, Sam Ahkeah also took up residence in Window Rock, and the tribal council instituted an executive committee, also called an advisory committee, to consider important local issues. Over the next few years, Ahkeah and other prominent Navajos, such as Jacob Morgan, testified before Congress about the urgent need for improved roads, schools, health care, and other concerns.

Congress responded by passing the Navajo-Hopi Rehabilitation Act of 1950. This legislation was in keeping with the Termination era, for it was designed to encourage the Navajos to take charge of their own economic development. Through this act, the tribe received $88 million over a ten-year period for internal projects. Almost $25 million was spent to construct schools, but even more was directed toward improving reservation roads and highways.

New and improved roads and highways gave the Navajos greater choice as to where they worked and shopped. Suddenly there were alternatives to the nearest trading post. As driving conditions improved, more tourists came to Navajo country, and after World War II tourism sharply boosted the tribal economy. The development of industries on the reservations, a goal strongly encouraged by the federal government, appeared feasible as road travel became easier. And, for better or worse, the isolation of most rural residents of the reservation was reduced. Although many communities were still difficult to reach, especially in the snowy winter months, a basic change had occurred in Navajo life.

Improved roads also allowed Navajo children more access to schools. If they were to survive and prosper, the Navajos knew, their children and young adults needed better education. Returning veterans had come home to find that the majority of children on the reservation were not enrolled in school. In years past, children had been needed to help care for the sheep herds. But with an increasing number of adults becoming wageworkers, younger Navajos now had the time to attend school. New educational programs and new institutions had to be started quickly.

For the younger students, several alternatives existed. Some attended existing BIA or mission schools on the reservation, but there were too few of these institutions to accommodate all school-age Navajo children. During the 1950s, the BIA funded thirty-six temporary schools, housed in trailers and scattered across the reservation. These gradually enrolled more than a thousand elementary-school students. Yet even with these temporary schools, thousands of Navajo children—especially those over elementary-school age—had to board away from home. A few students attended existing BIA boarding schools off the reservation. During the 1950s, the tribal government also constructed student dormitories near towns just outside the Navajo Reservation, such as Gallup, New Mexico, and Flagstaff, Arizona; some teenage Navajo students lived in the dorms and attended the towns' non-Indian public high schools. But Navajo parents became more involved in their children's education, and they demanded more local schools.

The obvious answer was to develop a public school system on the reservation. But public schools are usually funded by state governments using state tax revenues. The residents of federal Indian reservations, however, are exempt from state and local taxes. Because the Navajos did not pay property tax to Arizona, New Mexico, and Utah, the three states over which the reservation spread, these states' governments were unwilling to build and run reservation schools. Another source of funding had to be found.

In 1950, Congress passed two laws authorizing federal aid to public school districts that educated the children of military personnel. Three years later, these laws were amended to finance the construction and operation of schools on Indian reservations as well. This federal funding made it possible for the Navajos in the 1950s to begin to build the core of a public school system inside the reservation boundaries. For the first time, thousands of Navajo children were able to attend school and still return home to their families at night. But even after a nucleus of about twenty schools was completed, many students living in the most remote areas of the reservation were still forced by distance to attend boarding schools.

The Navajos also made efforts to improve educational opportunities for young adults who had not attended school as children. In 1946, a special five-year program was created by the BIA for students too old to take classes at the early elementary level. Off-reservation boarding schools—such as the Sherman Institute in Riverside, California, and the Intermountain School in Brigham City, Utah—also enrolled

During the 1950s and '60s, the lumber industry became an important part of the Navajo economy and Navajo Forest Products Industry (NFPI) ran the largest lumber mill in the Southwest. Unfortunately, by the 1980s most of the lumber on Navajo land had been harvested and NFPI was mired in debt.

many older Navajo students. These schools offered instruction in English and vocational training in such skills as welding, auto mechanics, and upholstering.

Most of the money for these programs came from the U.S. government, but another source of funds was found in the mid-1950s when natural resources were again discovered on Navajo lands. Oil companies renewed their interest in the region, and in 1956–57, large oil and gas fields were found on the reservation near an area called Four Corners, where the borders of Arizona, New Mexico, Colorado, and Utah meet. This discovery was a great boom to the Navajo economy. Navajo oil royalties soon ran into the millions of dollars each year. With these funds coming in to the tribal treasury, the council began to think more ambitiously about funding its own institutions.

Money from newly exploited uranium deposits also added to the tribal funds. During World War II, an enterprise called the Vanadium Corporation had begun mining uranium on reservation lands. Interest in atomic energy grew rapidly after the war, and consequently so did Navajo revenues. In 1950, the tribe earned $65,000 in uranium money; in 1954, the amount had increased tenfold—to $650,000. At the same time, the tribe was also earning money by carefully managing its own lumber industry.

In 1969, through a tribal council resolution, the Navajos would begin officially to call themselves the Navajo Nation. That resolution was able to come about because of the development born in the 1950s, a decade when the Navajos at last possessed both the financial resources and the determination to take charge of their destiny. In the face of federal and public efforts to assimilate the Navajos, the people grew all the more determined to assert their dual identity as Navajo Americans.

During the 1950s, through the leadership of Tribal Chairman Sam Ahkeah and his successor, Paul Jones, and the hard work of many others, the Navajos made numerous other significant improvements in reservation life. New chapter houses were built. A tribal college-scholarship program was created. The court system was revamped, and the council was given power to appoint seven judges for life terms. The tribal government was expanded to deal with wider responsibilities. The *Navajo Times*, a reservation-wide newspaper written in English, was established. In 1958, a tribal sawmill became the basis of the Navajo Forest Products Industry (NFPI), and the following year the Navajo Tribal Utilities Authority (NTUA) was founded. Despite the many challenges the Navajos faced by the end of the 1950s, they had built a solid base on which to construct their new nation.

7

The Navajo Nation

The 1960s, 1970s, and 1980s were an extraordinary period in Navajo history, an era marked by optimism and confusion, cohesion and controversy. Through it all, the Navajos clearly emerged as major participants in Southwestern society and in national American Indian life. Between 1960 and 1990, the Navajo population doubled, soaring to about 200,000. By 1990, the tribe remained the largest in the United States and occupied more than 25,000 square miles of land. Despite progressive innovations in such areas as legal aid, health care, and industry, many ancient cultural traditions remained lively. Yet troubling questions about the Navajos' future persisted.

Navajo education was one sphere that saw enormous development. By the mid-1960s, four types of schools existed in Navajo country: mission schools, BIA boarding and day schools, public schools, and contract schools. The last of these were run by employees hired by locally elected school boards that were granted at least partial funding for these institutions through contracts with the BIA.

Over the course of the 1960s, the BIA's direct role in Navajo education declined. On-reservation boarding schools served primarily students from the reservation's most remote areas. During the end of the decade, the BIA did open new elementary boarding schools in the Arizona communities of Chuska, Toyei, and Many Farms, and new boarding high schools in Many Farms and Tuba City. At the same time, however, it closed some older, smaller schools. On the whole, the percentage of Navajos attending BIA schools decreased. Off-reservation boarding high schools, which had at one time enrolled hundreds of students, were nearly all shut down.

The Navajos' dissatisfaction with BIA schools, especially boarding schools that cut children off from their parents and community, led to the push for contract schools. Although these were dependent largely on the BIA for funding, the Navajos had greater control over what was taught in their classrooms. The Navajos' first contract school was Rough Rock Demonstration School, which opened in 1966.

Rough Rock, an isolated community in the heart of Navajo country, proved an ideal location for this pioneering venture. Although the local school board members themselves had little formal education, they were well known and respected in the community, which gave the school great support. Most Rough Rock residents were traditionalists who raised sheep, traded at the local post, and spoke Navajo as their first language.

The board hired Robert Roessel, the white husband of a Navajo woman, as Rough Rock Demonstration School's first principal, and he in turn hired its teaching staff. Roessel had taught for many years in various Navajo schools, and under his charismatic leadership, the school at Rough Rock quickly gained national attention. Native history, culture, and language received much more emphasis at the new school than in any

BIA institution. In the fall of 1968, Roessel relinquished his post to a Navajo, Dillon Platero.

Rough Rock Demonstration School soon served as a model for similar institutions in other communities, such as Rock Point School in Arizona, and Ramah School and Borrego Pass School in New Mexico. The Rough Rock school's Navajo Curriculum Center proved particularly influential. The center published and distributed innovative educational materials—such as primers written in both Navajo and English—which employed traditional stories and examples drawn from Navajo life. Using these, teachers encouraged students not only to speak Navajo but to learn how to read and write it.

In the 1960s and 1970s, following the example of the relatively few contract schools, many state-run public schools departed from their old goal of completely integrating Navajo students into the mainstream culture. At this time, more and more Navajo children began to attend public schools, thanks to improved roads and the relocation of many families into towns or their environs, where wagework could be found. In turn, more Navajos gradually registered to vote and elected increasing numbers of Navajo school board members, who insisted on new school policies that were more in keeping with Navajo values. Navajo parents were, of course, as divided as any group of non-Indian parents about what constituted the best schooling for their children. But as parental involvement in schools increased, so did the quality of elementary and secondary education available to all Navajo students.

Increased Navajo control did not, however, in itself solve some deep-rooted problems of their educational system. Low salaries, frequent turnover of personnel, and student dropout rates higher than the national average remained serious concerns. Nevertheless, more Navajos became teachers and administrators at reservation schools, which gave Navajo children role models whom they could respect and emulate.

With help from the tribal scholarship fund and other

Diné College, located in Tsaile, Arizona, was founded in 1968 and was the first college in the United States established by Native Americans for Native Americans. Shown here is the Ned A. Hatathli Culture Center, which is named for the first Navajo president of the college.

grants, loans, and programs, record numbers of Navajos began to attend colleges and universities. These included the state universities of Arizona, New Mexico, and Utah, as well as private institutions such as Brigham Young University in Provo, Utah. Many graduates returned home to work as lawyers, teachers, or professionals trained in other areas.

Because not every deserving Navajo student was able to leave the reservation, the tribal council in 1968 founded Navajo Community College (NCC)—the first community college established on an Indian reservation. Originally located at Many Farms, NCC's permanent campus opened in 1973 at Tsaile, Arizona, and a branch campus opened later at Shiprock,

New Mexico. The college, which graduated its first students in 1970, offered associate degrees based on two-year programs; one degree, for example, was in bilingual-bicultural education. Courses were also taught in traditional subjects, such as weaving, and NCC's arts and crafts program eventually produced skilled silversmiths as well.

In 1972, the United Presbyterian Church founded a second on-reservation postsecondary institution, the College of Ganado, at Ganado, Arizona. This school, like NCC, offered two-year programs toward an associate degree, but it stressed a more conventional curriculum. Some students from the Hopi and other Southwestern Indian reservations also attended Ganado. A number of Ganado and NCC students went on to receive a bachelor's degree from a four-year university, but in September 1986 Ganado itself—never a very large school—closed its doors for lack of funds and students. However, NCC immediately moved to convert part of the Ganado campus to its own use.

Just as education boomed in the 1960s and 1970s, legal representation became more available to Navajos at this time. In the late 1950s, legal help was first offered to Navajo individuals by several Legal Aid Service lawyers hired by the tribe. But there were too few lawyers to meet the people's overwhelming needs.

In 1963, Lyndon B. Johnson became president and soon announced that the federal government would wage a "war on poverty" in the United States. As part of this program, the Johnson administration created the Office of Economic Opportunity (OEO) in Washington, D.C. Funds from the OEO helped to establish the Office of Navajo Economic Opportunity (ONEO) on the Navajo Reservation. One of ONEO's most popular programs was its legal service, which was popularly dubbed Dinebeiina Nahiilna be Agitahe (Navajo for "attorneys who contribute to the economic revitalization of the people") and soon shortened to DNA.

DNA rapidly hired eighteen law-school graduates, opened

offices in several towns, and took on a variety of cases. These dealt with workmen's compensation claims, landlord-tenant problems, divorce suits, misdemeanor offenses, grazing rights disputes, and more. Given DNA's willingness to confront controversial issues, its future did not look promising, but because it helped so many people, it proved to be a valuable resource.

Federal funding of DNA and its parent was part of a new national policy toward American Indian groups. Called self-determination, it sought to encourage tribes to take control of their own economic well-being by funding programs to promote economic growth on reservations. Among other ONEO ventures at this time were the establishment of a small-business development center, an extensive preschool teaching program, a recreation program, a Neighborhood Youth Corps (which involved thousands of teens), and a Home Improvement Training program. Millions of dollars of federal money were allocated to these programs, and Navajos soon filled most of ONEO's administrative positions. Heading ONEO was a man who would subsequently dominate Navajo political life for more than a generation, Peter MacDonald.

Born December 16, 1928, in the reservation community of Teec Nos Pos, Arizona, MacDonald grew up speaking Navajo and learning traditional ways. As a teenager, he enlisted in the Marine Corps and became one of the youngest Code Talkers. After World War II, he resumed his education at Bacone High School in Oklahoma. In 1957, he earned a B.S. in electrical engineering from the University of Oklahoma. MacDonald worked for six years as a project engineer with Hughes Aircraft in southern California. In 1963, he returned to the Navajo Reservation and gained a position with the tribal government. After helping to draft some Navajo management plans and a successful request for federal funds, he became—by a tribal board appointment—director of ONEO in May 1965.

In this position, MacDonald quickly assumed center stage

in the drama of Navajo public life. For five years, MacDonald directed, with high visibility, heavily funded programs, such as DNA, that had a widespread impact on the Navajo Nation. People soon came to associate him with these generous, Navajo-run efforts. In 1970, MacDonald resigned from ONEO to run for tribal chairman against incumbent Raymond Nakai.

MacDonald's assets included familiarity with federal funding methods, a traditional background combined with off-reservation experience, and a history of close contact with the Navajo people while heading ONEO. Nakai emphasized to voters his achievements as tribal chairman, including improved education, purchases of new land for the reservation, and the establishment of new industry.

How best to develop industry without depleting Navajo resources or disrupting traditional ways was an important question during the election. Expansion of the Navajo economy had been a perennial challenge to the tribal council and chairman. Most Navajos did not want to leave their homeland. Yet job prospects were limited, especially for those with little education or training. Livestock raising, *agriculture*, tourism, and traditional crafts would support only a limited number of people. The tribal government itself, local schools, and federal government agencies all offered employment to those qualified, but clearly greater opportunities were needed. The reservation's geographic isolation and the scarcity of seed money had long deterred local residents from starting new businesses. Consequently, in the early 1960s, the Navajos had decided to try to take better advantage of the reservation's natural resources. They tried to persuade non-Indian-owned, well-capitalized companies to come onto the reservation and not only pay for whatever resources they used but also train and employ Navajos.

At the start of the 1960s, oil revenue continued to inflate the tribal treasury. But coal and uranium mining also became major new sources of income. The rapidly growing population of California and the Southwest had created a market for these fuels. The developing regional economy desperately needed new energy sources.

In 1962, Utah Mining and Manufacturing signed a contract with the Navajos that allowed them to strip-mine coal from land south of the San Juan River in New Mexico. Adjacent to this land, the Arizona Public Service Company constructed an electricity-generating facility, the Four Corners Power Plant. Later, in 1964 and 1966, the tribal council also agreed to lease lands on Black Mesa for strip mining by the Peabody Coal Company and to allow a power plant to be built at Page, Arizona. All these agreements were negotiated by Chairman Nakai and the council to boost the tribal funds and create jobs. At the time, however, most council members did not fully realize how much damage strip mining and coal-fired plants could cause.

Strip mining involves the removal of successive layers of earth from a vast expanse of land to get at the mineral deposits underneath. Once the deposits are exhausted, only a vast, barren open pit remains. The refining of the raw deposits also requires large quantities of water, a scarce resource in Navajo country. Finally, the burning of the refined coal itself at the power plants generates an alarming amount of air pollution. Aside from a concern for the damage this did to the tourist industry, many Navajos also agonized that they were selling their very birthright for a short-term gain. They feared that after the resources—and the companies that needed them—were gone, their land would be forever destroyed.

But these increasingly controversial, resource-depleting enterprises were not the only ones to locate on Navajo land during the Nakai administration. The Navajos sought to lure other large-scale industry with cheap land leases, favorable construction arrangements, and a trainable work force. Two major firms accepted the Navajos' invitation: Fairchild Semiconductor and the General Dynamics Corporation. These

In the 1960s, the Navajos leased land on their reservation to the Peabody Coal Company, which used a process known as strip mining to mine the coal on Navajo land. This mining process, which is very damaging to the environment, removes coal from successive layers of earth until all the deposits are exhausted.

manufacturing concerns, however, yielded fewer jobs and less tribal income than the people had initially hoped.

Another major concern at the time of the Nakai-MacDonald contest was the joint-use land area shared with the Hopi tribe, whose own reservation was entirely surrounded by that of the Navajos. Problems over the joint-use area dated back to the original 1882 executive order; they had grown of increasing concern to the Navajos as questions arose not simply over grazing rights but also over mineral and even occupancy rights. When the Hopis won exclusive occupancy rights in a court case, Navajos regarded the decision as a major defeat, and longtime tribal attorney Norman Littell was ousted not long thereafter. MacDonald charged Nakai's new tribal attorney, Harold Mott, with being inexperienced in Indian law and exceeding his authority.

Navajos responded to the court's ruling with resistance. While many Navajos eventually relocated under duress, the residents of Big Mountain in northern Arizona refused to vacate their land. Big Mountain came to be associated with Navajo refusal to move and make way for the Hopis. Further, the most vocal voices against relocation were the elderly matriarchs at Big Mountain.

In the election of November 1970, MacDonald received nearly three votes to every one cast for Nakai. In his inaugural address the following January, the new tribal chairman pledged:

> What is rightfully ours, we must protect; what is rightfully
> due us, we must claim. . . . What we depend on from others,
> we must replace with the labor of our own hands and the
> skills of our own people. . . . What we do not have, we must
> bring into being. We must create for ourselves.

MacDonald pledged not to "barter away the Navajo birthright for quick profit" and further argued that the tribe must no longer "depend on others to run our schools, build our roads, administer our health programs, construct our houses, manage our industries."

The Navajo government under the MacDonald administration promptly took on a more aggressive attitude. At the chairman's urging, the Navajos hired new legal counsel, the Phoenix-based firm of Brown, Vlassis and Bain. One partner, George Vlassis, served as the tribe's primary attorney. In 1971, the tribal council created a Navajo Division of Education, which subsequently started a teacher education program to increase the number of Navajo instructors. The next year, the Navajo Housing Authority was formed to build and manage tribal housing with money from the U.S. Department of Housing and Urban Development (HUD). At MacDonald's invitation, the AFL-CIO labor union federation set up a worker training program that helped decrease tribal unemployment. Voter registration drives boosted the Navajos' political clout, especially in Arizona, forcing non-Indian politicians to pay attention to local interests. Finally, MacDonald instituted the renegotiation of old gas and oil leases on terms more profitable to the Navajos.

The tribe's economic problems were not easily solved, however. In the 1970s, an attempt to develop Navajo uranium resources resulted in protests that echoed those made earlier against coal extraction. In a joint venture that made the Navajos partners rather than employees, Exxon agreed to pay the tribe $6 million for uranium exploration rights in northwestern New Mexico. The Navajos hoped to gain millions more from the actual operations. But once again, controversy erupted. Local residents complained bitterly that they had not been consulted. Concerns escalated as reports surfaced about the poor health of Navajo uranium miners who had worked in the area of Grants, New Mexico. The highly publicized closing in 1979 of the Three Mile Island nuclear power plant near Harrisburg, Pennsylvania, caused further worries about the safety of nuclear power. Such concerns, combined with plummeting market prices for uranium ore, left the proposed joint venture in oblivion as of the late 1980s.

During most of this period, the Navajo Forest Products Industry (NFPI) had a more positive image. Based in the community of Navajo, New Mexico, NFPI represented Navajo control and careful management of the tribe's forests. By the late 1970s, it had more than six hundred Navajos on its payroll and indirectly employed hundreds more. A falling timber market nationally would present new problems for the operation in the 1980s, but generally NFPI's record reflected a successful use of this resource, which—unlike oil and coal—was both "clean" and renewable.

Unfortunately, another effort modeled after NFPI proved

less productive. The Navajo Agricultural Products Industry (NAPI) had been created in April 1970 to operate a 100,000-acre farm. This land was to be irrigated as part of the Navajo Indian Irrigation Project, which had long promised to deliver water to the Navajos from the San Juan River in New Mexico. Although the participants—including Bahe Billy, a Navajo agriculturalist who had earned his doctorate at the University of Arizona—were dedicated to making NAPI work, the project was often mismanaged and suffered major financial setbacks. Disputes also arose from allegations that some individuals were being allowed access to NAPI land because of their influence in reservation politics. Because of these problems, only part of this land would later be irrigated.

Such disputes were indicative of the greater problem of uncertain water rights, a severe drawback to economic development on the reservation. In theory, the Navajos possessed important water rights, but in practice they exercised very little of this potential power. The Colorado River and other sources of water are already oversubscribed. A court victory by the Navajos could represent a crucial breakthrough, but in a region where little rain falls, the Navajos face formidable non-Indian competition for this particularly precious resource.

Throughout his campaign against Raymond Nakai and during his first term in office, MacDonald had repeatedly promoted Navajo self-determination. He contended that Navajos needed to open more of their own businesses so that they could stop relying so heavily on wages from non-Indian employers and welfare from the government. Navajo entrepreneurs responded to his call by establishing small businesses. Gas stations owned or leased by Navajos would later dot the reservation. One Navajo man, Don Davis, opened a Chevrolet dealership in Tuba City, Arizona, in December 1978. The tribal government also continued to promote tourism with enthusiasm. Canyon de Chelly, Monument Valley, and other natural wonders attracted growing numbers of foreign and American visitors.

Canyon de Chelly, which the U.S. government established as a national monument in 1931, is comprised entirely of Navajo Tribal Trust Land. Located near Chinle, Arizona, the area that surrounds the monument has been home to Native people, including the Navajos, for more than 1,500 years.

A number of communities also established cooperative businesses. An early example was the Pinon Co-op. It was founded in 1971 in Pinon, Arizona, partly as an alternative to trading posts, which continued to be run largely by non-Indians. The Pinon Co-op sold groceries, gasoline, and dry goods, and subsequent cooperative ventures offered feed for livestock as well. Credit unions and arts-and-crafts cooperatives also provided Navajos with the opportunity for community-based, mutually beneficial endeavors.

During his first term, MacDonald appeared to provide bold new leadership for the Navajos. He challenged them to raise their ambitions and to develop a more assertive posture in dealing with the reservation's non-Indian neighbors. He out-lined goals for the future and projected confidence that the people could meet these goals. In 1974, MacDonald won reelection by a comfortable margin.

By the early part of his second term, however, the chairman had lost the solid support he once enjoyed. His critics charged that, despite MacDonald's rhetoric of self-determination, the Navajos' situation had not actually changed. In 1975, the reservation suffered a disturbing, though relatively minor, fiscal setback after Fairchild Semiconductor cut employment at its reservation plant because of a nationwide economic recession. When members of the American Indian Movement (AIM), a militant political group, seized the plant in protest, Fairchild responded by shutting down the long-ailing plant—permanently.

More damaging to MacDonald was a scandal that wracked the Navajo Housing Authority (NHA). In February 1976, Arizona senator Barry Goldwater demanded a federal audit of the tribal government, following rumors of corruption. An NHA official ultimately pleaded guilty to charges involving misuse of more than $13 million in housing funds. In 1977, MacDonald himself was indicted by a Phoenix grand jury on the allegation that he had submitted false invoices to a utility company. The chairman hired criminal lawyer F. Lee Bailey for his defense, and the jury was unable to reach a verdict on the eight federal charges against him.

Despite the damaging publicity that resulted, MacDonald was reelected in 1978, again by a three-to-one margin, because the other candidates split the votes of those who opposed him. His election to three consecutive terms was unprecedented in Navajo politics. Indeed, MacDonald looked unbeatable at the polls until four years later, when a candidate of comparable stature entered the race for the chairmanship. In Peterson Zah, director of DNA, MacDonald finally faced a rival who ran the type of campaign he himself had waged against incumbent

Raymond Nakai in 1970. Zah defeated MacDonald and served as tribal chairman from 1982 to 1986.

Originally from Low Mountain, Arizona, and a graduate of Arizona State University, Zah at first seemed capable of holding on to the chairmanship for more than a single term. But MacDonald retained a considerable following in certain chapters, and events seemed to conspire against Zah's success. Perhaps foremost among these was the continuing land dispute between the Navajos and the Hopis. A judicial decision proclaimed that Navajos living in the contested area were to be relocated elsewhere. Although the number of residents to be removed was reduced in subsequent haggling, as was the amount of acreage to be surrendered, the final result was widely seen as another Navajo loss. MacDonald's militant stance played well with the Navajo public, in contrast to Zah's moderate public tone. The chairman was also criticized for his inability to work out an agreement with his former schoolmate, Hopi tribal chairman Ivan Sidney. Zah's popularity suffered as well from a general slowdown in the Navajo economy during his years in office. In actuality, this stemmed largely from cutbacks in federal aid that the tribe was powerless to prevent. Nonetheless, Zah bore the brunt of Navajo dissatisfaction over the recession.

As a result, the 1986 tribal election was a bitterly contested race. Peterson Zah actually carried three of the five Navajo electoral districts, but Peter MacDonald soundly defeated the incumbent elsewhere. When the votes were tallied, MacDonald had won election to a fourth term by a margin of 750 votes out of some 61,000 cast.

But Peter MacDonald's return to power was troubled from the very beginning. Within a month of taking office, the chairman ordered the *Navajo Times* closed down. His reasoning was that the newspaper was losing money, but his opponents claimed it was because the paper had been persistently critical of MacDonald. A few months later, the *Navajo Times* resumed publication on a weekly basis.

The chairman's troubles were just starting, however. In the middle of his fourth term of office, MacDonald became the center of political turmoil when, during hearings of the U.S. Senate Select Committee on Indian Affairs in January 1989, he was accused by Navajo and non-Navajo witnesses alike of receiving kickbacks—specifically, of benefiting personally from the tribal government's purchase of a ranch of nearly a half million acres south of the Grand Canyon. The tribal council soon placed its chairman on administrative leave; and the following month, MacDonald conceded on KTNN Radio, a Navajo station in Window Rock, that he had indeed taken "gifts" from individuals seeking business deals with the reservation. "Yes, I have accepted gifts," he told listeners, according to a subsequent newspaper account. "But that is not a crime."

This revelation divided the Navajos into two factions. In the absence of a formal tribal constitution, both pro- and anti-MacDonald groups claimed control of the government. Ultimately, in an attempt at compromise and conciliation, the tribal council appointed an interim chairman to serve out the remainder of MacDonald's term: Leonard Haskie, a council member from Sanostee, New Mexico, who was comparatively unknown outside the Navajo reservation. Despite this appointment, political marches and demonstrations continued. In July 1989, two Navajo men were killed and several other people injured when a pro-McDonald rally erupted into a violent confrontation with Navajo tribal police. With this event, it became clear that, regardless of who eventually retained government control, years would pass before the political shock waves died down.

Optimistic observers expressed the hope that the Navajos might at least emerge from this political struggle with a renewed sense of national purpose. But the Navajo Nation was far more than a political entity. It represented a unique people who together had survived the misery of the Long Walk, the confinement at Fort Sumner, and the trauma of livestock

Three Navajo children sit in the back of a pickup truck on the reservation. In today's world, Navajo parents and educators recognize the importance of teaching their children the culture and language of their people.

reduction. There could be no doubt that the Navajos would endure.

As the Navajos prepared for the twenty-first century, they continued to blend change with continuity. A significant percentage of the people still spoke the Navajo language, practiced traditional ceremonies, and honored old values. A justifiably proud people with a rich heritage, they continued to gain strength from their home territory. Within the four sacred mountains, the Navajos would try, as Barboncito foretold so many years ago, to remain as happy and as prosperous as the land.

8

The Navajos in the Twenty-First Century

On June 1, 1999, hundreds of Diné (the People) and their supporters gathered at Northern Arizona University in Flagstaff, Arizona, to celebrate Treaty Day, a day Navajo leaders set aside to commemorate the treaty signed in 1868 between Navajo leaders and the United States. The treaty had traveled from the National Archives in Washington, D.C., to Flagstaff, where thousands of Navajos were able to view the document. Sight of the treaty unleashed a flood of stories passed down through Diné memory. While the People remembered the nightmare of the 1860s, when the United States subjugated their ancestors, they also told stories of how their ancestors had made sacrifices so that the People could return to their beloved homeland and begin the process of rebuilding their lives.

In 1968, Chairman Raymond Nakai marked the one hundredth anniversary of the Navajos' return from Bosque Redondo. The return

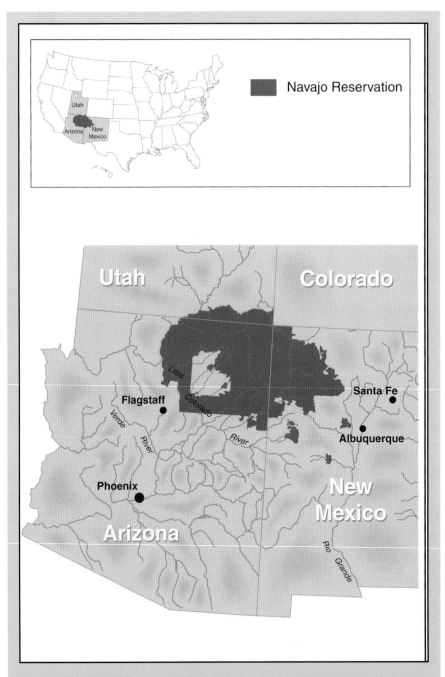

The Navajo Nation spreads over portions of Arizona, New Mexico, and Utah, cover-
ing more than twenty-five thousand square miles.

of the 1868 treaty to Dinétah afforded yet another opportunity for Navajos to note the strides made as they entered the twenty-first century. In the 1990s, Navajos sought to resolve some of the problems they had encountered with the onset of the modern age, while at the same time dealing with emerging isssues. Most importantly, the People endeavored to keep Diné philosophy at the center of their lives, from their government, to their communities, to their families.

While many Diné might raise questions about the extent to which their government is founded upon traditional principles and call upon their leaders to return to tradition, there is little doubt that Diné values are still very much a part of social, cultural, and educational life. The resilience in keeping Diné ways holds steadfast as the People continue to look to them to shape their lives and as they strive to pass on the knowledge of the ancestors to the next generation. Today, traditional knowledge is passed on in numerous ways that reflect the colonial encounter: Navajo citizens blend Diné ways with American thought and practices but with the goal of remaining Diné.

In the 1940s and 1950s and through the 1980s, Navajo leaders had embraced the promise that the development of their natural resources would bring prosperity to the Navajo Nation. Instead, in the 1990s, Navajos faced the growing possibility that coal mines could close. Importantly, they realized that Peabody Coal was depleting the precious underground water supply, which the company was using to transport coal to the Mohave station near Las Vegas, Nevada. Efforts to get compensation for uranium miners and their families, begun in the 1980s, continue as Navajo leaders seek reform to national uranium compensation initiatives so that more Navajo miners will be eligible.

Realizing that revenues from mining natural resources would soon end, Navajo leaders looked to other sources, such as gaming, to replenish the tribal treasury. Acting to change communities for the better, the establishment of Kayenta Township gave Diné citizens a chance to see how economic development could work. Leaders also considered the settlement of Navajo water rights. Additionally, the long hard years of struggling with the conflict over the land with the Hopis in northern Arizona continued as a handful of Navajos refused to sign seventy-five-year accommodation agreements with the Hopi government.

The 2000 U.S. Census indicated that once again, the Navajo population had increased—the population was 275,000. Of the 180,000 persons who resided within the boundaries of the Navajo Nation, 175,000 were Navajos. More than 100,000 Navajos lived in urban areas, such as Phoenix and Flagstaff, Arizona; Albuquerque, Gallup, and Farmington, New Mexico; and Barstow and Los Angeles, California. The census also showed that the Navajo population is young, with the median age between eighteen and twenty-four. Interestingly, of the Native Americans who filled out the census forms, more than 90 percent of Navajos identified themselves as Navajo only. In contrast, other Native Americans noted that they were of mixed heritage. Further, the census gave an indication that Navajos, like the rest of Americans, were becoming urbanized. The growth of towns like Window Rock, Fort Defiance, Tuba City, Shiprock, and Kayenta in Dinétah has meant a transformation in the cultural landscape as more and more Diné look for wage work in communities, nearby towns, and government centers. Living in urban areas has also meant easier access to schools, shopping centers, and activities such as basketball. Such a transformation has also raised troubling questions about the importance of Navajo values, such as the place of livestock—a means of livelihood that Navajos have traditionally imbued with much meaning.

The 1989 struggle for power between pro- and anti-Peter MacDonald supporters highlighted the consequences of not having a formal tribal constitution. As a result of the problems with MacDonald's administration, the Navajo Nation government took measures to reduce the president's power by passing a landmark resolution amending Title II of the tribal code on December 15, 1989. The reforms created the position of a speaker of the house, who would preside over the Navajo Nation Council. The reforms also decreased the number of standing committees and removed from the president the power to appoint members to legislative committees and gave it to the speaker of the council.

In further movements toward government reform, when Albert Hale was elected president in 1995, he called for a return of power to the Navajo people. The Navajo Nation Local Governance Act in 1998 gave chapters a chance to participate in decisions of local importance. Early in his presidency, however, Hale was charged with ethical violations, including spending tribal money inappropriately, accepting bribes, and having an affair with his press secretary. Amidst these allegations, Hale stepped down. The government reforms that decreased the president's power seemed to be working as Hale left office without the conflict that had ensued when the tribal council forced Peter MacDonald from office.

With Albert Hale's removal from office, several interim presidents served. Thomas Atcitty served only four months after being accused of accepting gifts from corporations. Milton Bluehouse then took over the presidency. In 1998, fourteen people declared their candidacy for president. LeNora Y. Fulton, council delegate from Fort Defiance and the second woman to run for the highest office in Navajoland, was one of the contenders. Fulton's decision to run for president raised discussion among Navajos about whether a woman should lead the largest Indian nation in the United States. Some Navajos felt that a woman should not be leader, citing a traditional story to validate their opposition. According to this story, during primordial times, a woman became a leader and chaos had ensued. Fulton addressed the contention by arguing that traditional stories also convey the significance of both male and female roles for the People's survival. Although Fulton was not successful in her bid, her candidacy brought

Urban Diné

The 2000 U.S. Census reported that approximately 75 percent of Native Americans live in U.S. cities. Navajos make up a sizeable population of those who have migrated to urban America. According to National Indian Youth Council Director Norman Ration, the Navajo population in Albuquerque, New Mexico, is probably one of the highest—at 48,000—while in Phoenix, Arizona, the Navajo population is reported at 24,000.

Until fairly recently, Navajos, like other urban Natives, have been not only invisible but seen as having lost much of their traditional practices and their own language. Today, we know that many urban Navajos maintain ties with kin who live on Navajo land and that they strive to keep their cultural practices alive. While urban Navajos have been invisible in mainstream America and unrecognized by their own tribal government, their voices are increasingly being heard.

At the end of the 1930s and into the 1940s, Navajos were forced into the wage economy because of livestock reduction. Many men left their reservation homes in search of jobs. They found employment in Arizona mines and in agricultural fields in California and in the Midwest. They also found labor jobs with the railroad. Women found work in the service industry and often worked in white middle-class homes as domestics. These types of jobs allowed them to return home for short periods where they could participate in ceremonies and help with the spring planting and the fall harvesting.

In the 1950s, federal Indian policy terminated some tribes to begin the process of moving Native peoples into the American mainstream. The U.S. government also enacted a relocation program and moved Navajo families into urban areas, where they were given assistance in finding jobs, and counseling so they could adjust to city living. Navajo students were given financial assistance for enrolling in schools where they could learn practical trades.

attention to women in leadership roles throughout Indian society.

Although Navajos still might disagree on whether a woman

Both Albuquerque and Phoenix are a short drive from Dinétah, so Navajos often return home on the weekends and on holidays. In addition to taking their part in extended family responsibilities, they also have necessary ceremonies and prayers conducted for their families and themselves.

In 2003, Navajo President Joe Shirley, Jr.'s office announced that the Navajo Nation had appropriated $300,000 to Navajos in Phoenix who have organized and established Diné Phoenix, Inc. In Albuquerque, similar efforts are being made to create an organization that will act on behalf of urban Navajos. Perhaps in the near future, two chapters will be created in the aforementioned cities and bring the number of chapters from 110 to 112.

No longer willing to be unrecognized or invisible, especially by the Navajo Nation government, which does not extend privileges that Navajos on Navajo land take for granted, urban Navajos are demanding access to funding set aside for health, education, and adequate housing. As Norman Ration points out, the Navajo Nation counts urban Navajos in their census and uses these numbers to apply for federal funding that tribes are eligible for. However, urban Navajos have not received any of the financial and economic benefits that other Navajos have received.

Given the realities of life on the Navajo Reservation, where jobs are scarce, education opportunities are limited, and housing is still inadequate, the migration into cities will continue. However, emerging urban Navajo leaders are demanding improved living and working conditions for their constituents and holding the Navajo Nation accountable to all Navajos. Contrary to the intentions of the relocation policies of the 1950s, urban Navajos retain strong identities as Navajos and look to their own cultural practices for sustenance and renewal.

Annie Wauneka, shown here in a 1963 photograph, served on the Navajo Tribal Council from 1951 to 1981 and was awarded the Presidential Medal of Freedom in 1963 by President Lyndon B. Johnson. Wauneka, who died in 1997, was the daughter of Henry Chee Dodge, the founding chairman of the Navajo Tribal Council.

can lead the Navajo Nation, they do acknowledge that women have skills and talents that are important to Navajo society. Annie Wauneka was elected to the tribal council in 1951 and served for the next thirty years. Often the sole woman on the tribal council, Wauneka served as a role model for women who aspired to public office. Wauneka's achievements include the eradication of diseases such as tuberculosis on the reservation, which led President Lyndon B. Johnson to present the Presidential Medal of Freedom to her in 1963, the highest civil honor an individual can be awarded during peacetime. In the twenty-first century, the number of women elected to the council is slowly growing.

Women demonstrate excellence and, especially, use their talents and skills for the benefit of their communities. Moreover, while the Navajo Nation has yet to elect a woman president, several women have been named to prominent positions in the 1990s and into the twenty-first century. Cassandra Manuelito became the first woman president of Diné College, the first tribal college established in the United States. Dorothy Lameman Fulton became the first woman chief of police for the Navajo Nation. The Nation confirmed Claudeen Bates Arthur as the first woman chief justice to be appointed to the Navajo Nation Supreme Court. Like their male counterparts, Navajo women draw upon traditional stories for leadership qualities and guidance. They believe that their roles are crucial to the Navajo people's survival.

Some of the most vocal resisters at Big Mountain in northern Arizona are women. Today, they remain at the forefront of the resistance, as U.S. government officials declare deadlines for the final removal of all Navajos from Hopi partition lands. In 1996, Congress enacted Public Law 104-301, the Navajo-Hopi Land Dispute Settlement Act, which implemented the Accommodations Agreement. The Act ratified the settlement of four claims of the Hopi Nation against the federal government and authorized the Hopis to exercise jurisdiction over the land awarded to them earlier. The Accommodations Agreement provided an avenue for Navajo families to remain in their homes. Each accommodation agreement allowed for three acres plus ten acres of farmland. Grazing rights depended upon a permit from the Hopi tribe. The leases were not transferable and only good for the duration of the original signer's life, although in some cases, the Hopis will consider renewing a lease for another seventy-five years. Five hundred and seventy Navajos signed the agreement that allowed them to stay on Hopi partitioned lands for seventy-five years. The agreement also called for the U.S. government and the Navajo Nation to pay the Hopis more than $50 million as part of the settlement. To date, the U.S. government has spent more than $330 million to move more than 9,000 Navajos and approximately 100 Hopis.

Today, a handful of Navajos still live at Big Mountain, on Hopi partitioned land, and refuse to sign the Accommodation Agreement. On March 31, 1997, yet another deadline for the complete removal of Navajos from Hopi partitioned lands passed. In the summer of 2001, in an effort to force Navajos out of the area, Hopi officials destroyed a Sun Dance ceremonial ground at Big Mountain, saying that the Navajos were using the ceremony as a political tool and that they were illegally squatting on Hopi land.

On April 23, 2002, Navajo elder Roberta Blackgoat died. She became nationally recognized when she refused to relocate from land upon which she had been born and where she had raised her children. Her warnings about mining's destruction of the land have been taken seriously by grassroots organizations such as Dineh Biziil coalition. In 1978, during the initial phases of the dispute between Hopis and Navajos, Thayer Scudder, an expert on relocation of rural populations, testified before Congress that the Diné would suffer great hardships if they were forced to leave the only homes they had ever known. Today, stories of great stress, including psychological and emotional distress, and of the debilitating consequences of forced relocation circulate among the Navajo people. Newlands, one area where Navajos were relocated, near Sanders, Arizona, was recognized in 1992 as a new chapter called Nahata Dziil. This new chapter was built according to urban plans, where homes are placed within close proximity to each other and where livestock is not allowed, a hardship for many Navajos who depend upon livestock for their livelihood.

The relocation controversy has followed the mining of Black Mesa, which many of the area residents have criticized. Peabody Coal Company opened its strip mines in 1970 and has relied on Navajo and Hopi water to move 5 million tons of coal

A crane mines coal at Black Mesa on the Navajo Reservation. Strip mining has been a point of contention for Navajos because it has created hundreds of jobs and generated millions of dollars of income for the tribe, but it has polluted the air and water on the reservation.

annually to the Mohave station near Laughlin, Nevada. From the Kayenta strip mine, which is not far from the Black Mesa mine, Peabody moves 7 million tons of coal annually by conveyor belt 17 miles to storage silos near Black Mesa. From there, the coal is shipped eighty miles to the Navajo generating station near Page, Arizona. Over the years, Navajo area residents have complained about the effects that the mines have had on their quality of life. In addition to being forced to move to make way for mines, they observe that little effort has been made to reclaim mined land, and that the air and water are polluted. Today, Navajos are troubled by the ongoing exploitation of their land, but they are also equally concerned about the jobs that will be lost if the mines close. The mines have pumped billions of dollars into the Navajo and Hopi economies through employee salaries, lease payments, mining royalties, tribal taxes, charitable donations, and scholarships.

The last few years have seen growing concerns among local Navajo and Hopi residents who assert that Peabody's use of more than a billion gallons of water per year is depleting the water supply. Navajos and Hopis note that land struggles might have alienated them across tribal lines, but the fight to stop Peabody from continuing its use of pristine underground water has united them. The Navajos and Hopis belong to various grassroots organizations, such as Black Mesa Trust, Black Mesa Water Coalition, To'Nizhoni Ani, and Natural Resources Defense Council, that have emerged to oppose Peabody's use of water drawn from the underground aquifer known as the Navajo or N-aquifer. Young educated Navajos like Wahleah Johns and Enei Begay share information and resources with Vernon Masayesva, the director of Black Mesa Trust and the former chairman of the Hopi tribe. Nicole Horseherder and her husband founded To'Nizhoni Ani and rely on Navajo elders for their support. All of these people and their members are committed to one thing: Peabody must stop using their precious water to slurry coal. Ten years of continued opposition is forcing U.S. officials, including the secretary of the Interior, to scrutinize Peabody's mining operations. However, the Navajo and Hopi residents' insistence that Peabody cease using pristine water to slurry the coal has not been realized.

In the 1940s and 1950s, the Bureau of Indian Affairs encouraged Navajo leaders to accept leases with corporations to open Navajo land to uranium mining. Initially seen as a boost to the economy, in which Navajo men could get jobs to support their families, by the 1980s, many Navajos realized that they had paid a high price for allowing uranium mining on their land. The Kerr-McGee Company, the first corporation to mine uranium on Navajo land, found conditions to their advantage. At the time, there were no taxes, health, safety, or pollution regulations, and few other jobs existed for Navajos returning from service in World War II.

Navajo uranium miners hauled radioactive uranium ore out of the earth as if it was coal. They drank the water as they ate their lunches in the mines. Sometimes they made their homes out of the radioactive waste, and their sheep watered at the small ponds that formed at the mouths of abandoned mines. On dry, windy days, the gritty dust from uranium waste tailings covered everything in sight. By the 1960s, nearly two hundred miners had died of uranium-related causes; the number of deaths doubled by 1990. Reports of Navajo babies with birth defects and Down's syndrome, both of which had been unknown before the mines opened, began to emerge in the 1990s.

In 1996, Timothy Benally, a former uranium miner, was named the director of the Navajo Uranium Workers Program, which was established in 1990 to identify former Navajo miners and to assist them in dealing with the Radiation Exposure Compensation Act Public Law 101-426 (RECA). RECA was to pay compassionate compensation to uranium miners who had worked during the Cold War era of 1947 to 1971. The program proved to be useful as Navajo miners found that because of their traditional practices and their limited access to quality medical care, they did not fit the criteria established for compensation. The miners and their families continue to wrestle with the consequences of uranium mining, including the need to change the criteria for RECA so that more retired Navajo miners qualify for compensation.

In 2005, the Navajo Nation considered a resolution to end all uranium mining on Navajo land. The Diné Natural Resources Protection Act will prohibit conventional uranium mining and place a long-term moratorium on uranium processing. The resolution would stop Hydro Resources, Inc. (HRI) and the company's proposal to mine four areas near the communities of Crownpoint and Churchrock, New Mexico.

Navajos who have formed a citizens group, the Eastern Navajo Against Uranium Mining (ENDAUM-CCT), lobbied the council to approve the resolution.

The prospect of mines closing brought about the realization that an important source of revenue would eventually disappear. In the 1990s, in efforts to improve economic opportunities, Indian nations looked to gaming. While many of the tribes have created successful casinos and put the profits toward improving their communities, others have not fared as well. In 1994 and 1997, the Navajo Nation Council put gaming referendums before Navajo voters. Both times, Navajos rejected gaming. Many Navajos oppose gaming because traditional beliefs link gaming with excess and immorality. Navajos also worried of the negative consequences of gaming, especially as the casinos would rely on Navajo clientele. Not deterred by the rejection, council delegates moved forward with plans to establish casinos and proposed a gaming ordinance to President Kelsey Begaye, which he signed. One of the first locations most likely to have a casino will be Tóhajiilehí (formerly Canyoncito), just twenty-five miles west of Albuquerque. The proposed 100,000-square-foot casino will not serve alcohol. Consultants have estimated that the casino will realize a net profit of $55 million by the fifth year of operation. Many Navajos remain troubled about the consequences of gaming, and issues have to be worked out, especially as Tóhajiilehí residents are seeking to retain 90 percent of the profits for their own community, with only 10 percent going to the Navajo Nation.

Another development that shows promise for the Navajo Nation is the establishment of the Kayenta Township. Navajos still face chronic unemployment, poverty, and all of its accompanying ills, such as a shortage of housing. On November 5, 1985, the Navajo Tribal Council withdrew 3,606 acres of Navajo trust lands to create the Kayenta Township. For decades, citizens have been critical about the lack of development and civic management on Navajo land. Finally, after years of endless procedures and political wrangling, the Kayenta Township was formally established when the Navajo Nation Council passed a resolution to create the Kayenta Retail Sales Tax Project. In November 1985, the council authorized an election for voters living within the township boundaries to elect commissioners. In 1997, Jimmie Austin, Jerry Gilmore, Yazzie Leonard, Richard Mike, and Charles Young were elected to the Kayenta Township Commission. In the first eighteen months, the tax brought in $670,834. Residents began to see improvements, including the construction of a post office, a waste transfer station to take care of the dumping and trash problem, and the ongoing establishment of a three-hundred-home subdivision. Even today, in other parts of Navajoland, similar improvements need to be made because problems such as trash dumping into ravines remains widespread. Adequate housing also remains a formidable obstacle for Navajo families. The Kayenta Township is a development that has generated enthusiasm for the rest of the Navajo Nation, even as some Navajos feel that urban living challenges traditional Navajo life, as it de-emphasizes the raising of livestock.

On December 29, 2004, after three years of review, the Navajo Council passed a resolution that would settle Navajo claims to the San Juan River. The attempts to settle Navajo water rights are not without opposition and controversy. In one of the first council deliberations to consider the issue, delegate Hope MacDonald-Lonetree from Tuba City reminded her fellow delegates that the Navajo Nation was a sovereign entity that should not give away its water rights simply to quiet non-Indians who contest Navajo rights. Her father, Peter MacDonald, also voiced his opposition in a commentary published in the *Navajo Times*. MacDonald, who was released from a federal prison in 1999, after serving seven years of a fourteen-year sentence, urged Navajo leaders and the community to retain water rights. As he noted, the Winters Doctrine recognizes Navajo rights before

The Navajo Tribal Council is made up of 88 delegates, representing 110 local units of government throughout the Navajo Nation. The delegates meet at least four times a year at the Navajo Nation capital in Window Rock, Arizona.

other claimants to the water. Navajo citizens such as Peter June Cordell wrote letters to the *Navajo Times* and argued that leaders should not settle for less than what the Nation was entitled to. In a council session where the delegates considered the settlement of water rights, some delegates walked out after opponents called for a debate; delegate MacDonald-Lonetree insisted that her fellow delegates look at the document and have it read into the record.

Finally, on December 22, 2004, after several hours of having the water rights settlement read into the record, the council voted to accept the resolution that would quiet Navajo water rights. The San Juan River Settlement recognizes the Navajo Nation's right to more than 606,060 acre-feet (cubic feet) of diverted water annually (about 56 percent of the total available for use) and will provide $800 million from the State of New Mexico to build the Navajo-Gallup Water Supply Project by December 2020—providing municipal water to chapters in the eastern and central areas of Navajo land. The settlement does not include funding to complete the canal system for the Navajo Indian Irrigation project, a project that was supposed to be completed under an earlier water rights settlement agreement made in the 1970s. Water would also be supplied for the Fruitland-Cambridge Irrigation Project, the Hogback-Cudei Irrigation Project, and several other smaller irrigation projects. These projects benefit Navajo farmers who live close to the San Juan River in the northern portion of Navajoland. Each year they plant corn, watermelon, and squash to sell on the Navajo market. Many of them plant hay for feed. They may also have a few sheep and goats.

The Diné way of life is shaped by federal, state, and tribal government in many ways. However, the People take individual initiatives to claim Navajo tradition as important in their lives. Although they never forget the hardships their ancestors endured, they do not allow themselves to dwell on the past. After expressions of sadness and mourning, they shake themselves out of it and tell stories of regeneration, for it is the Diné way to look to the future with hopes for harmony and balance. Relying upon the ancient teachings embedded in *Sa'a naghái bi'ke'hózhó* (or hózhó), the Path of Life to Happiness and Old Age, as Navajo philosophy has been translated, the Diné strive to reclaim traditional practices that sustained their ancestors.

Although Navajos still regard sheep and other livestock as central to their lives, in fact, fewer and fewer families keep livestock. Most have a few sheep, goats, cows, and horses, but it is usually enough to remind them that these animals teach important values about life. One place that Navajos remind themselves about sheep's value is through weaving. The art of weaving is a significant manifestation of a tradition that was given to them by Grandmother Spider. Historically, Navajo women have been renowned for the beauty and artistry of their weaving. Textiles that were initially woven for everyday wear quickly became coveted trade items that hosts of Spaniards, Mexicans, and then Americans remarked upon throughout the late eighteenth and early nineteenth centuries. By the end of the nineteenth century, the textiles that Navajo women spent so many laborious hours weaving were no longer made for Navajo use but were popularized as rugs and wall hangings for collectors and tourists who began to flood into the Southwest after the 1880s and into the twentieth century. Navajo women, for the most part, have lost control of the sales of their textiles. Instead, traders who began to control the rug industry after 1868 are still in charge. As many weavers have reported, and as anthropologist Kathy M'Closkey confirms, weavers see very little return for their labor.

Navajo women continue to weave, and more recently, men have come into the public eye as skilled weavers in their own right. While the market for Navajo-made textiles might ebb and flow, weavers continue to turn out spectacular textiles that rival those made by their grandmothers. In attempts to take control of the textile market, in some areas of Navajoland, weavers have created cooperatives and established auctions, such as the one that takes place in Crownpoint, New Mexico. Bonnie Benally Yazzie is the director of the Eastern Navajo Weavers Association. She spends many hours teaching weaving to anyone who is willing to learn. Mothers and daughters take Benally's instructions as a way to return to cultural values and to renew their mother-daughter bonds. At auction time, Benally educates buyers about the textiles they are buying and about the threat that weavers face as knock-offs from Mexico and overseas flood the market, making it difficult for weavers to get fair value for their handmade products.

Given that women have not seen sufficient financial returns for their labor—although there are a few weavers who are nationally renowned for their textiles—one has to wonder why women continue to weave. Many weavers explain to outsiders that weaving has been very important for the survival of their families. In many cases, weavers have contributed significantly to the well-being of their families by using their earnings from rug sales to put food on the table and to buy school clothes for their children. If asked, a weaver may offer the meaning of the textiles beyond economics, for weaving is also infused with a deep cultural significance that spans from the weaver to her family to her extended and clan kinships to the natural world.

While there is still a question as to the role that formal education should play in relaying Navajo values, in communities, and as part of their daily lives, many Diné share their knowledge of traditional ways in hopes that the teachings of the ancestors will prevail. Significantly, while many Diné attended education institutions where Diné teachings were either a small part of or nonexistent in the curriculum, they often returned home and relearned the Diné way. Many claim the responsibility to relay ancient Diné lessons in a variety of avenues, such as schools and conferences. Others work as consultants who teach the traditional narratives and skills, such as weaving.

In the 1990s, more Bureau of Indian Affairs schools came under local community control. While local control is viewed as a positive step toward reclaiming Navajo education, a web of schools is still overseen by various federal, state, and tribal administrations. As a result, Navajo studies as part of curricula is still sporadic. The Navajo language is also not consistently taught anywhere within the Navajo Nation. In 2005, under President Joe Shirley, Jr., the Navajo Nation Council is considering education reforms that would establish Navajo control over all schools on the Navajo Reservation, regardless of whether the school is run by the state, the federal government, or the Navajo Nation. The call to establish a department of education is a response to New Mexico and Arizona reports that Navajo students, like many of their non-Indian counterparts throughout the area, are failing national standards that all students should

Joe Shirley, Jr., was elected Navajo president in 2003. The native of Chinle, Arizona, hopes to institute educational reforms that would give the Navajos control over all the schools on their reservation, regardless of whether the school is run by the state or the federal government.

meet to graduate from high school. The creation of a department of education will unify the curricula taught in all schools on Navajoland and set education standards that match those of New Mexico and Arizona. A school board based in Dinétah would oversee all of the schools.

Navajos might find it a challenge to prepare their students for the twenty-first century, but they have made significant inroads. The wisdom of the Navajo Tribal Council to establish a scholarship fund in the late 1950s has born fruit. Students who took advantage of the scholarships returned home to work in their communities as teachers, leaders, social workers, business people, artists, writers, engineers, and council delegates. Many have embraced the call to return to tradition as part of their responsibility to the People. In myriad ways, they use their education, talents, and skills to promote and preserve traditional values through contemporary forms shaped by exposure to modern American society.

In 1964, Taylor McKenzie was the first Navajo to attain a medical degree. In 1994, Lori Arviso-Alvord became the first Navajo woman to be board certified in surgery. In her autobiography, *The Scalpel and the Silver Bear*, Arviso-Alvord tells her story of growing up on the reservation. She attended Crownpoint High School in the 1970s, became interested in the sciences, and went to medical school at Stanford University. Today, as the Associate Dean for Student and Minority Affairs at Dartmouth Medical School and assistant professor of surgery, Dr. Arviso-Alvord is dedicated to finding ways to integrate Western medicine with Navajo philosophy.

While Fred Begay was the first Navajo to earn a Ph.D. in Physics from the University of New Mexico in 1971, Karletta Chief, a doctoral student at the University of Arizona, continues a tradition of excellence as she works toward a Ph.D. in Hydrology. Chief put her education on hold for a year when she won the Miss Navajo Nation title for 2000–2001. During her reign, Miss Chief spoke of the need to use Western education for Navajo benefit. Her Ph.D. will allow her to participate in discussions where Native Americans and Navajos must make decisions about environmental issues surrounding coal and uranium mining, and Navajo water rights. As Navajos recall, the great nineteenth-century Navajo leader Manuelito declared that the People must use American education for their benefit. Alvord and Chief are inspired by their leader's wisdom.

Diné writers Luci Tapahonso, Laura Tohe, Esther Belin, and Irvin Morris use contemporary forms to convey traditional knowledge to a receptive Navajo audience, many of whom belong to a growing younger population. They experiment with prose, poetry, and sometimes music to offer portrayals of contemporary Navajo life with all of its trials and tribulations.

Grandmothers and grandfathers, children and babies, rodeo cowboys, and boarding schools appear in stories that paint colorful Navajo lives. The authors do not flinch from the hardships and sufferings that Navajos have experienced under colonialism. Their stories have the power to move their audience to appreciate and value cultural practices.

Other Navajos literally go into communities to convey the value of Navajo teachings and practices to parents and children. In an effort to bring about an appreciation for Navajo values, Marilyn Help coauthored a book, *We'll Be in Your Mountains, We'll Be in Your Songs: A Navajo Woman Sings*, with University of New Mexico professor Ellen McCullough-Brabson. As a young woman, Help won the Miss Navajo title, among several other pageant titles. With the achievements that came with representing the Navajo people as Miss Navajo under her belt, Help went on to raise her family and attain a bachelor's degree in elementary education. Today, Help is busy with her teaching duties at Fort Wingate Elementary, where she teaches Navajo studies. When not teaching, she travels and shares her expertise in Navajo culture with Navajos who have a yearning to learn. On the weekends, she can be found at kinaaldas—the age-old puberty ceremony that Navajo families still conduct for their daughters who have come into womanhood—where she oversees the making of the enormous corn cake that will be placed in a pit for overnight baking. Help, like so many Navajos, finds that a return to Navajo tradition is a way to ensure the continuity of the People.

The Diné, like their grandmothers and grandfathers once did, also embrace certain American cultural traditions and practices that are easily integrated into their way of life. In particular, American sports such as basketball, cross-country skiing, golf, and rodeo are favorites in many Navajo communities. Perhaps because it is easy to put up a basketball hoop outside a home where everyone has access to the game, basketball is a favorite sport that draws crowds at local high schools. Many

Radmilla Cody, like Karletta Chief and Marilyn Help, is a former Miss Navajo Nation. The Grand Falls, Arizona, native is a well-known singer and has released Navajo versions of "God Bless America" and the "Star Spangled Banner."

high school teams compete successfully and go on to state championship games that take place in Phoenix, Arizona, and Albuquerque, New Mexico. Not deterred by the hundreds of miles required to travel to games in cities, fans follow their favorite teams and fill the gyms to capacity. Few colleges recruit Navajo athletes and even fewer athletes make it to the professional circuit. But when they do, athletes like Ryneldi

Becenti draw huge Navajo and Native American fans. Becenti played basketball for Arizona State University. In 1992, she was the leading scorer on a team that won twenty games. With Becenti on board, the team won a bid to play in the NCAA Tournament for the first time in nine years. When Becenti played for ASU, the white basketball players could not help but comment on the Navajo fans who often filled the gym to capacity; prior to Becenti's membership on the team, the women often played in nearly empty gyms. Becenti went on to play for the U.S. team in the World University games in 1993. Rainy Crisp, another Navajo woman, also played for Arizona State. Today, Navajo athletes, in addition to Becenti and Crisp, are making an impact in a number of sports. Two notables are golfing pro Notah Begay III and racecar driver Cory Witherill.

The People have successfully incorporated many aspects of American culture into their own society, and at the same time, they remain very much Navajo. Like other Americans, they, too, have been consumed by the unfolding national events precipitated by September 11. On September 11, 2001, America was shocked by Osama bin Laden's attack on the Pentagon in Washington, D.C., and the World Trade Center in New York City. President Bush's call to attack Afghanistan and Iraq in retaliation was answered by many Americans who joined the military, including Navajos. At present, approximately one thousand Navajo men and women serve in the U.S. armed forces. These latter-day warriors explain that, in enlisting in the U.S. military, they follow a tradition set down by their grandparents who defended their country and their land. As of early 2005, three Navajo men—Duane Todacheene, Harry Shondee, Jr., and Quinn Keith—have lost their lives in the war in Iraq.

The war in Iraq is just one example of how the Diné see their dual roles as Navajo and American citizens (they are also citizens of states such as New Mexico and Arizona). They are proud to be Navajos who have preserved a distinct cultural heritage and proud to be Americans who are concerned about the welfare of the United States. Like other Americans, the war is just one issue they are debating. They are also considering questions that President Bush's administration has raised, including the ban on same-sex marriage, the meaning of the No Child Left Behind Policy, and the consequences of privatizing social security. In addition to settling these questions, the Navajo Nation will examine taxation as a way to replace dwindling finances, define the role that urban Navajos—primarily those who live in Phoenix, Arizona, and Albuquerque, New Mexico—will play in the Navajo Nation, and how they will deal with budget cuts that the Bush administration is proposing, which could be potentially devastating for all Indian nations. Through all of these troubling questions about the future, of both the American nation and their own Navajo Nation, they value the beliefs that helped guide the way for their ancestors through both good and bad times.

The Navajos at a Glance

Tribe   Navajo

Culture Area   Southwest

Geography   Colorado Plateau country of northeastern Arizona, northwestern New Mexico, and southeastern Utah

Linguistic Family   Athapaskan

Current Population (2000)   Approximately 275,000

First European Contact   Probably Antonio de Espejo, Spanish, 1582

Federal Status   Recognized. The Navajo Reservation includes aproximately 32,000 square miles of land. It is located primarily in Arizona and extends into New Mexico and Utah

A.D. **1400**   By this year, Navajos settle in what is now the American Southwest.

1582   Spaniard Antonio de Espejo becomes first European to encounter the Navajos (in northwestern New Mexico).

1626   Spanish Franciscan friar Zarate Salmeron recognizes Navajos as distinct tribe.

1630s   Spanish Franciscan friar Alonso de Benavides remarks on the skill of the Navajos as farmers.

1630s–1860s   Spanish and later Mexicans carry out slave raids against the Navajos.

1680   Navajos participate in the Pueblo Revolt, driving Spanish from Pueblo territory.

1706   First peace treaty between Spanish and Navajos.

1749   Spanish establish Catholic missions of Encinal and Cebolleta in Navajo country; some Navajos are exposed to Christianity, but the missionaries are quickly driven out.

1772   Navajos and Gila Apaches establish an alliance to fight against the Spanish.

1786   At this time, Navajos are divided into five groups: Canyon de Chelly, Cebolleta, Chuska Mountain, Ojo del Oso, and San Mateo.

1821   Mexico declares independence from Spain.

1846   U.S. Colonel Stephen Kearny claims Santa Fe, New Mexico, as territorial capital for United States; Navajos and U.S. officials meet at Fort Wingate, New Mexico, to establish peace.

1848   Treaty of Guadalupe Hidalgo ends war between United States and Mexico—under its terms, more than 1.2 million square miles of territory are ceded by Mexico to the United States for $15 million; Navajos and other tribes of the Southwest are placed under U.S. jurisdiction.

1849   Treaty signed between U.S. government and the Navajos; this treaty along with one signed in 1868 are the only two of nine signed between the federal government and the Navajos that were ratified by the U.S. Senate.

1853   Henry Linn Dodge named first Navajo Indian agent.

1855   Manuelito named chief of Navajo tribe.

1860   Manuelito and Barboncito lead attack on Fort Defiance in New Mexico Territory.

1863   U.S. government decides to relocate Navajos to an area known as Bosque Redondo (round grove, in Spanish), near Fort Sumner on the Pecos River in what is now east-central New Mexico.

1864   Many Navajos die on the Long Walk, the 250-mile march to the Navajo reservation at Bosque Redondo.

1866   Manuelito surrenders and many Navajo leaders, including Barboncito, quickly follow suit.

1868   Navajos and U.S. government sign treaty that establishes initial boundaries of Navajo Reservation in northwestern New Mexico (about one-fourth of the tribe's traditional territory).

1878–86   Navajo Reservation is increased in size by five major land annexations.

1882   Presidential executive order establishes a 2.4 million acre reservation for the Hopis, which forms the basis for the Navajo-Hopi land dispute.

1884   Henry Chee Dodge named head chief of the Navajos.

1921   Oil discovered on Navajo land.

1922   U.S. government creates Navajo Business Council, which includes Chee Dodge, Charlie Mitchell, and Dugal Chee Bekiss. The men are supposed to represent their people in negotiating oil leases with the United States.

1932   Thomas Dodge, Chee's son, is elected tribal chairman.

1934   Navajos reject Indian Reorganization Act; congressional legislation adds 243,000 acres of land to Navajo Reservation, including the Hopi village of Moencopi.

1934–1940s U.S. government carries out livestock reduction program.

1940 Navajos pass resolution banning the use of peyote on reservation lands; Native American Church, which uses the drug in its ceremonies, holds that the resolution violates the First Amendment. In *Native American Church v. Navajo Tribal Council* (1959), federal court holds that the First Amendment does not apply to Indian nations.

1941–1945 More than 3,500 Navajos serve in World War II.

1942 Chee Dodge elected tribal chairman again.

1950 Congress passes the Navajo-Hopi Long Range Rehabilitation Act, which authorizes more than $88 million to be spent addressing economic, education, health, and social concerns of both tribes.

1958 Congress passes Public Law 85-547, which calls for the Navajo and Hopi Tribal Councils to participate in a lawsuit that would determine which tribe holds rights to land, as set forth in the 1882 treaty.

1962 Navajo Tribal Code published.

1963 Raymond Nakai elected Navajo tribal chairman.

1970 Peter MacDonald elected Navajo tribal chairman.

1974 Congress passes Public Law 93-531, giving the U.S. District Court of Arizona the authority to evenly divide the Joint Use Area (JUA) between the two tribes.

1977 As a result of the partitioning of the Joint Use Area, 3,495 Navajos are forced to relocate, compared to only 40 Hopis.

1982 Peterson Zah elected Navajo tribal chairman.

1986 Original deadline for Navajos to have been relocated as stated by Public Law 93-531.

1987 Peter MacDonald elected for an unprecedented fourth term as tribal chairman.

1989 Amendments to Navajo Tribal Code call for office of tribal chairman to be split into speaker of the council and president.

1990   Congress passes Public Law 101-426, which provides compensation to many Navajo uranium miners.

1994   Presidential executive order calls for June 1 to be designated "Navajo Nation Treaty Day."

1996   Congress passes Public Law 104-301, the Navajo-Hopi Land Settlement Act, which gives Hopi tribe 75-year leasing authority over Navajos who live on their designated land.

1999   Kelsey Begaye elected tribal president.

2003   Joe Shirley, Jr., elected tribal president.

GLOSSARY

agriculture—The science, art, and business of soil cultivation, crop production, and the raising of livestock.

anthropology—The study of the origin and the physical, social, and cultural development and behavior of humans.

archaeology—The recovery and study of evidence of human ways of life, especially that of prehistoric peoples but also including that of historic peoples.

assimilation—The absorption of a culturally distinct group into the prevailing culture.

Athapaskan languages—A group of related languages spoken by Indian peoples whose ancestors were native to the region of Lake Athapaska in northwestern Canada. Among the languages in this group are those of the Navajos, the Hupas, and the Mescalero Apaches.

barter—The practice of trade without the exchange of money.

Blessingway rite—The core ritual of the Navajos' traditional religion. Variations of this ceremony can be performed for any number of purposes, including the protection of livestock, the blessing of a marriage, or the protection of warriors from their enemies.

Bureau of Indian Affairs (BIA)—A U.S. government agency established in 1824 and assigned to the Department of the Interior in 1849. Originally intended to manage trade and other relations with Indians and especially to supervise tribes on reservations, the BIA is now involved in programs to encourage Indians to manage their own affairs and improve their educational opportunities and general social and economic well-being.

chantways—Navajo rituals performed to heal or protect a person, presided over by a singer who fulfills the functions of both doctor and priest.

clan—A multigenerational group that has in common its identity, organization, and property and that claims descent from a common ancestor. Because clan members consider themselves closely related, marriage within the clan is strictly prohibited.

Code Talkers—A group of several hundred Navajo men who were selected by the Marine Corps during World War II to send coded messages to Pacific battlefronts. The Navajo language served as the basis for the code, which was instrumental in defeating the Japanese.

culture—The learned behavior of human beings; nonbiological, socially taught activities; the way of life of a given group of people.

Diné—The Navajo word meaning "The People." This is the term the Navajos use to refer to themselves.

Dinétah—The Navajo word meaning "The Land of the People." The term is used by the Navajos to refer to what is now northwestern New Mexico.

drypaintings—Also called sandpaintings, these images are made with dry pigments such as sand and corn pollen by a helper, under the supervision of a singer, for use in some of the curative Navajo ceremonies. Drypaintings range in size from less than 1 foot to more than 20 feet in diameter. After the ritual, the drypainting (usually of a sacred figure or symbol) is destroyed.

hogan—A cone- or dome-shaped dwelling with a frame made of logs and bark and covered with a thick coat of mud. Navajo families lived in hogans that usually measured between twenty and thirty feet in diameter.

hózhó—The Navajo word meaning beauty, happiness, harmony, and goodness. It summarizes the basic goal and ultimate value of the Navajo world.

Indian Claims Commission (ICC)—A temporary federal court created by an act of Congress in 1946 to hear and rule on claims brought by Indians against the United States. These claims stemmed from unfulfilled treaty terms, such as nonpayment for land sold by the Indians.

Indian Reorganization Act (IRA)—The 1934 federal law that ended the policy of allotting plots of land to individuals and provided for political and economic development of reservation communities. Self-government was permitted, and tribes wrote their own constitutions for that purpose.

kinaalda—The four-day ceremony conducted for a Navajo girl when she reaches puberty. During the kinaalda, female elders instruct the girl in what her duties and responsibilities as a Navajo woman will be.

linguistics—The study of the nature, structure, and history of human speech and languages.

Long Walk—The grueling 250-mile journey of more than 8,000 Navajos to the Bosque Redondo area in east-central New Mexico Territory in 1863–64. The U.S. Army compelled the Navajos to leave their homeland and relocate to Bosque Redondo after conquering them in battle. The Navajos were allowed to return to their homeland five years later according to the terms of their 1868 treaty with the federal government.

matrilineal descent—A principle of descent by which kinship is traced through female ancestors; the basis for the Navajos' clan membership.

GLOSSARY

mission—A ministry commissioned by a religious organization to promote its faith or carry on humanitarian work.

Native American Church—A religious organization whose practices combine elements of Christianity with rituals of traditional Indian religions. Many of these rituals involve the consumption of the hallucinogenic peyote cactus.

origin story—A sacred narrative that the people of a society believe explains the origin of the world, their own institutions, and their distinctive culture.

peyote—A cactus native to the southwestern United States and northern Mexico. The buttons of the cactus are sometimes eaten as part of Indian religious ceremonies.

reservation—A tract of land set aside by treaty for the occupation and use of Indians; also called a reserve, in Canada. Some reservations were for an entire tribe; many others were for several tribes of unaffiliated Indians.

Termination—The policy that sought to end the federal government's financial responsibilities to tribes and gradually to withdraw its special protection of reservation lands. The goal of this policy was to have individual states assume these responsibilities for the Indians who resided within their boundaries. It was thought that termination policy would encourage the integration of Indians into mainstream American society.

tribe—A community or group of communities that occupies a common territory and is related by bonds of kinship, language, and shared traditions.

Books

Alvord, Lori Arviso. *The Scalpel and the Silver Bear: The First Navajo Woman Surgeon Combines Western Medicine and Traditional Healing.* New York: Bantam, 2000.

Bailey, Garrick, and Roberta Glenn Bailey. *A History of the Navajos: The Reservation Years.* Sante Fe, N.M.: School of American Research Press, 1986.

Belin, Esther. *From the Belly of My Beauty: Poems.* Tucson, Ariz.: University of Arizona Press, 1999.

Bighorse, Tiana. *Bighorse the Warrior.* Edited by Noel Bennett. Tucson, Ariz.: University of Arizona Press, 1990.

Bingham, Sam, and Janet Bingham, eds. *Between Sacred Mountains: Navajo Stories and Lessons from the Land.* Tucson, Ariz.: University of Arizona Press, 1984.

Correll, J. Lee. *Through White Men's Eyes: A Contribution to Navajo History (A Chronological Record of the Navajo People from Earliest Times to the Treaty of June 1, 1868).* 6 vols. Window Rock, Ariz.: Navajo Heritage Center, 1979.

Iverson, Peter. *The Navajo Nation.* Albuquerque, N.M.: University of New Mexico Press, 1983.

———. *The Navajos: A Critical Bibliography.* Bloomington, Ind.: Indiana University Press, 1976.

———. *Diné: A History of the Navajos.* Albuquerque, N.M.: University of New Mexico Press, 2002.

Kluckholn, Clyde, and Dorothea Leighton. *The Navaho.* Garden City, N.Y.: Natural History Library, 1962.

M'Closkey, Kathy. *Swept under the Rug: A Hidden History of Navajo Weaving.* Albuquerque, N.M.: University of New Mexico Press, 2002.

McCullough-Brabson, Ellen, and Marilyn Help. *We'll Be in Your Mountains, We'll Be in Your Songs: A Navajo Woman Sings.* Albuquerque, N.M.: University of New Mexico Press, 2001.

PICTURE CREDITS

page:

3: Library of Congress, LC-USZ62-99571

7: Library of Congress, LC-USZ62-99572

12: © Pete Saloutos/CORBIS

17: Library of Congress, 15673

24: Image #2A-3635, American Museum of Natural History Library

29: © Academy of Natural Sciences of Philadelphia/CORBIS

36: © Bettmann/CORBIS

39: Smithsonian Institution

44: Smithsonian Institution

49: Library of Congress, LC-USZ62-99573

55: Milton Snow Collection, Navajo Nation Museum, Window Rock, AZ

60: BIA/Milton Snow Collection at Navajo Tribal Museum, Window Rock, AZ

69: Associated Press, AP

73: © Bettmann/CORBIS

78: Richard Erodes/Taurus

83: Richard Erodes/Taurus

88: Richard Erodes/Taurus

92: © CORBIS

96: Richard Erodes/Taurus

98: © Peter Lamb

104: © Time Life Pictures/Getty Images

107: © Jim Richardson/CORBIS

112: Earl Tulley

116: Associated Press, AP

119: Earl Tulley

A: Department of Material Culture, Colorado Historical Society, #CHS-X20038

B: Department of Material Culture, Colorado Historical Society, #CHS-X3002

C: Decorative and Fine Arts Department, Colorado Historical Society, #CHS-X3027

D: © AINACO/CORBIS

E: © George H.H. Huey/CORBIS

F: © George H.H. Huey/CORBIS

G: © Getty Images

H: © Getty Images

Cover: © Werner Forman/Art Resource, NY

Peter Iverson, Ph.D., is Regents' Professor of History at Arizona State University and taught at Diné College during its first years. Iverson is the author of several books on American Indians, including *Diné: A History of the Navajos, Carlos Montezuma and the Changing World of American Indians,* and *We Are Still Here: American Indians in the Twentieth Century.*

Jennifer Denetdale is the first Navajo woman to hold a Ph.D. in history. A native of Tohatchi, New Mexico, she is a member of the Diné (Navajo) Nation and is of the Zia and Salt clans. Denetdale is Assistant Professor of History at the University of New Mexico and has published articles in *New Mexico Historical Review, American Indian Culture and Research Journal,* and *Journal of Social Archaeology.*

Ada E. Deer is the director of the American Indian Studies program at the University of Wisconsin–Madison. She was the first woman to serve as chair of her tribe, the Menominee Nation, the first woman to head the Bureau of Indian Affairs in the U.S. Department of the Interior, and the first American Indian woman to run for Congress and secretary of state of Wisconsin. Deer has also chaired the Native American Rights Fund, coordinated workshops to train American Indian women as leaders, and championed Indian participation in the Peace Corps. She holds degrees in social work from Wisconsin and Columbia.